Charles H. (Charles Henry) Ross

There and Back one Shilling

Being Judy's Seaside and Holiday Book, for the Delectation.....

Charles H. (Charles Henry) Ross

There and Back one Shilling
Being Judy's Seaside and Holiday Book, for the Delectation.....

ISBN/EAN: 9783337211738

Printed in Europe, USA, Canada, Australia, Japan

Cover: Foto ©Andreas Hilbeck / pixelio.de

More available books at **www.hansebooks.com**

THERE AND BACK

ONE SHILLING.

BEING

JUDY'S SEASIDE AND HOLIDAY BOOK,

FOR THE DELECTATION OF ALL GAD-ABOUTS
AND SOME STAY-AT-HOME TRAVELLERS.

WITH HUNDREDS OF PICTORIAL PLEASANTRIES
By JUDY'S ARTISTS,

AND SOME PROSE
By CHARLES H. ROSS.

THE PROSE, WHICH HAS BEEN MANUFACTURED EXPRESSLY FOR
THIS WORK, IS NOW FOR THE FIRST TIME PUBLISHED.

LONDON:
PUBLISHED AT THE OFFICE OF "JUDY,"
73 FLEET STREET, E.C.

AT THE PAY PLACE.

SCENE—"THERE AND BACK" OFFICE, 73 FLEET STREET.

[JUDY *at the pigeonhole. To her enter hastily a* WOULD-BE TRAVELLER *with much luggage and a shilling.*

WOULD-BE TRAVELLER. "There and Back," if you please.

JUDY. One shilling.

WOULD-BE T. What class is it?

JUDY. It's all first-class.

WOULD-BE T. Till when is the return available?

JUDY. We do not desire its return. You may give it away when you have done with it, or, better still, keep it, and recommend all your friends to have a shillingsworth too.

WOULD-BE T. Can I insure against accidents?

JUDY. Not at this office. People making a purchase here frequently die of laughter before they get back again into the street.

WOULD-BE T. Good gracious!

[*Snatches up his purchase and makes for the door. Imprudently looks inside, and is found afterwards in a fit of laughter on the doorstep.*

June 15*th*, 1876.

THERE AND BACK.

PART I.

	PAGE
"TAKE YOUR PLACES!"	15
A Sad Case	16
A Little Incident	16
Catching the Train	19
The Old Way of Travelling and the New	24
Awful!	25
Seeing off Uncle Higgins	29
The Dream and the Awakening	34
The Vow of Vengeance	36
Then and Now	38

PART II.

AT THE SEASIDE	39
Shingles and Sand	42, 51
The Browns on their Travels	49
The Shop at Winklesea	57
"On a May-Day Morning Early"	63
"A bit worried"	92
About Wooden Spades	98
The Selfish Lover	98
A Bad Case	98
The Early Train	102
The Husband's Boat	102

PART III.

PROMENADES AND PIERS	105

PART IV.

SEASIDE AMUSEMENTS	113
Little Jones's Exhibition	116
Fishful Fancies	121
Bicycling Extraordinary	121

PART V.

BATHING	125
From between the Blankets	128
On the Unbecomingness of Mermaids' Attire	131

PART VI.

HINTS TO LODGING HUNTERS	139

PART VII.

ABOUT DINNERS	141
A Parting	148

THE "WANZER"
Lock-Stitch Sewing Machines.

"**L**ITTLE WANZER." Hand Lock-Stitch Sewing Machine.
500,000 in use.
Unequalled by any Hand Machine in the Market.

"**L**ITTLE WANZER." With Stand, to work by Hand or Foot.

"**L**ITTLE WANZER" is the Machine selected by the
National Board of Education for Ireland
As the only one to be used in their Seven Thousand Schools.
Beware of spurious imitations.

"**W**ANZER" A. New Hand Lock-Stitch Sewing Machine.

"**W**ANZER" A. Lock-Stitch Sewing Machine.
With Stand, to Work by Hand or Foot.

"**W**ANZER" F. New Family Machine.
With all the latest improvements

"**W**ANZER" F. Can be used for all Light Manufacturing Purposes.

"**W**ANZER" E. Lock-Stitch Sewing Machine,
With improved Wheel-Feed for Boot-Closing and Leather Work.
And with a special Foot for Heavy Tailoring.

CAUTION.—"Little Wanzer" **Sewing Machine**, Four Guineas.
Spurious imitations are being offered by unscrupulous dealers. Every genuine Machine is stamped with trade mark and address, 4, GREAT PORTLAND STREET, LONDON, W.

All the "**WANZER**" Company's SEWING MACHINES are Shuttle Lock-Stitch, and are guaranteed. Full particulars Post-free.

Chief Office : **4 GREAT PORTLAND ST.,**
LONDON, W.

Northern Depot: 58 BOAR LANE, LEEDS.

There and Back One Shilling.

"TAKE YOUR PLACES!"

AN EXCRUCIATING JOKE.

PASSENGER. *Two thirds to Ramsgate.*
CLERK. *Can't you say you want to go to Ashford? How should I be supposed to know how far two-thirds to Ramsgate is?*

[Passenger is flabbergasted, and Railway Clerks indulge in a roar at the witticism.

A SAD CASE.

"The trains to Notting Hill run every half-hour."—Information given by Company.
"Do they? Ha! ha!"—Remark by one who had tried them.

I SAW her but a moment,
   Yet, methinks, I see her still—
'T was at Victoria Station,
   And she wanted " Notting Hill."

Comes a " Notting Hill Gate " quickly—
   Comes one more, then one more still ;
But they suit not our poor maiden,
   For she wants a " Notting Hill."

That face, so wan and weary,
   Was sure enough to fill
With pity, heart of marble,
   In this case of Notting Hill.

I saw her but a moment,
   Yet, perhaps, she's waiting still—
Or, better still, has given up
   All hopes of " Notting Hill ! "

A LITTLE INCIDENT.

NIGGERS are proverbially thick-headed, but this is pretty nearly the thick-headest case on record.

When a new line was opened somewhere in America some time ago, an ancient negro, who lived in a cottage overlooking the rails, came out with a three-legged stool under his arm, and sat himself down between the rails of the up-line, so as to have a good fair stare at the first train that came along the down-line. It happened, though, that the train came on the up-line instead, and the ancient negro being rather in the way, hadn't proper time to turn round and have a good stare at the engine, and stoop and pick up his stool, and his umbrella and spectacle-case, and get out of the road before it was right up, and had bumped him over into a side ditch.

As a rule, this kind of thing happening to only a nigger wouldn't have been much consequence ; but the incident happening in the North just after the war, it was thought advisable to make an exception, and so they stopped the engine, and got down and looked into the ditch.

There was the nigger, sure enough—lying as flat as he could upon his face. They thought at first he was stone-dead, but he wasn't : he was hiding. So the engine-driver and the stoker got down into the ditch, too, and dug him out with their boots.

Then when they got him out, they put it to him as a man of sense, whether he thought he was going on at all reasonable? He didn't make any explanation on this point. He only said he was a poor man, and he hoped he'd not damaged the engine.

I myself don't believe this tale's true all through.

AN OLD BIRD *(with all his feathers on).* GUARD. Now, sir, take your seat, if you're going on! OLD BIRD. No, thank ye. You don't catch me riding alone with a lady.

SO STUPID OF HER! This is a poor dear old lady, three months after the close of the Hydrophobian Season, to whom the porter is explaining, just as the train is starting, that although what she has taken is a dog ticket she may not take the dog with her in the carriage, the Company, at the same time, does not hold itself in any way to the slightest degree responsible for its safe keeping in the luggage-van. And it is just possible that the train may start and leave her behind, long before she clearly understands what advantage there was in paying her money.

OPTIONAL.

LADY. *Can I take the train from here to London Bridge?*
TICKET INSPECTOR. *Well, I dare say you may try, if you like. The engine generally does.*

CATCHING THE TRAIN.

THE other day Thompson went to Ramsgate, and went by boat one Sunday, and took a return ticket. He had just thirty-five minutes allowed him to look round the town before the train started back again; and as he had not dined on board he had to get his dinner during the time, as well as see the sights.

It took him just fifteen minutes to make up his mind where he would dine, and then they kept him waiting twenty whilst they cooked his steak; and he got back to the pier just exactly seventeen and a half minutes after the boat had started, so he stopped in Ramsgate that night. In the morning the landlady called him early and gave him his breakfast, and told him if he looked very sharp indeed, he would just have time to catch the very latest train he possibly could catch, or be ruined for life!

When he left the house under these circumstances, he was naturally a little flurried, and ran out into the street and up to the end of it before he had time to think he ought to have asked the way first.

But at the end of the street he found a solitary man on crutches taking snuff, and tackled him:

ONE TO—SOMEBODY!

MINUTE WYKEHAMITE. *I say, you know! Dash it all, you know, where's my box I say?*

RAILWAY OFFICIAL. *Dash it all, sir, begging your parding, but were it an 'at-box or a pill-box, and was you inside on it, sir, when you last see it?*

"Which station might you want?" the man asked.
"How many are there?" asked Thompson.
"Well, there's only two as I know on," said the man.
"Well," said Thompson, "I want the one that goes to town."
"What town?" said the man.
"Well, London," said Thompson.
"Neither on 'em goes there to my knowledge," said the man, "but the train does."
"How do I get there?" said Thompson.
"You take one of the trains," said the man—"unless you go by the boat."
"I want the place where the trains start from," said Thompson.
"I don't think they'll let you have it," said the man: "it cost the company a lot of money."
"I want to know the way to the place where the trains start from to go to London," said Thompson.
"Which of 'em?" said the man. "Don't I tell you there's two?"
"I want to know the way to the nearest," said Thompson.
"There you have me!" said the man. "I've never rightly made up my mind which *is* the nearest from this spot where we're standing."
"Well," said Thompson, "let's have the way to either—choose yourself."
"No," said the man, "I shouldn't like to take the responsibility."
"Look here, confound you!" said Thompson, "will you, or will you not, tell me the way to a station, from which a train starts for London?"

OF COURSE.

ELDERLY AND ANXIOUS TRAVELLER. *Do you think the 12.50 train will be punctual, sir?*

PARTY ADDRESSED. *Well, I really can't say. It will be 10 to 1 if it is.*

"Look here, confound you!" said the man, "though I'm perfectly willing to impart all the information that lies in my power, I'm not a finger-post—so I just tell you!"

"I really beg your pardon most humbly," said Thompson; "and if you'll be good enough to direct me to the place I want to go to——"

"Which place *do* you want to go to?" said the man.

"Well," said Thompson, "if you'll give me the names of the two lines, I'll choose for myself, and we'll have no more words about it."

"Oh," said the man, "that seems a little bit more reasonable! There's the Chatham and Dover and the South-Eastern."

"Then," said Thompson, "I'll go by the Chatham and Dover; and if you will tell me the way to the station, I shall be very much obliged, because I'm in a hurry."

"You're in a hurry!" said the man. "Lord bless me! why didn't you mention that to begin with?"

* * * * *

Thompson lost the train, and was ruined for life.

ACCLIMATIZATION. SWELL (*to Guard, who has given the signal after a stoppage of half an hour*). I say, here—don't go on—let us out. We've taken quite a fancy to the place.

ANOTHER "WINDOW" FRACAS. HARMLESS SWELL. Would you—aw—object to having the glass down? no; in fact, I was on the point of asking you either to put your glass down or leave off staring at me!

RUFFIANLY YOUNG LADY. Oh, dear
SWELL. Aw!

CONSCIOUS!

GUARD (sternly). *Now, then, any more "going on" there?*
[But Brownsmith and the betrothed one need not have been so startled, there was nothing personal in the question.

THE OLD WAY OF TRAVELLING AND THE NEW

WHEN a certain Rory Random set out from a town some miles north of Newcastle-upon-Tyne on the first day of November, one hundred and thirty-six years ago, there was "no such convenience as a waggon" in that part of the country, and his finances were too weak to support the expense of hiring a horse; so he contracted with the carriers, and took his seat upon a pack-saddle between two baskets. But by the time he arrived at Newcastle, he was "so fatigued with the tediousness of the carriage, and benumbed with the coldness of the weather," that he resolved to travel the rest of his journey on foot, "rather than proceed in such a disagreeable manner."

But the hostler of the inn where he put up, understanding he was bound for London, advised him to take his passage in a collier, which would be both cheap and expeditious, and withal much easier than to walk upwards of three hundred miles through deep roads in the winter-time. Having, however, communicated

UNREASONABLE.

GUARD. *Now, then, my lad, LOOK SHARP!*

this idea to a friend, he did not approve of Rory's taking a passage by sea, "by reason of a winter voyage, which is very hazardous along that coast, as well as the precariousness of the wind, which might possibly detain him a long while—to the no small detriment of his fortune."

Eventually, however, he resolved to set out on foot and catch the Newcastle waggon, that had left for London three days before, which he was informed he could easily do, and which he did.

A brave old journey was that, I warrant me, which Doctor Tobias Smollett so amusingly describes, and lasted more days than I could venture to tell you. You may do your fifty miles an hour now, and have done nothing very wonderful. You may take your ticket any day, and be far beyond the place or destination you bargained for in ten minutes' time, if the signalman makes a mistake!

AWFUL!

MODESTY, as the poet has observed, is one of the brightest ornaments in woman's diadem. The other day a young female person, o'er whose brow some forty summers may have passed, was thrown into a state of the most painful confusion just after taking a second-class ticket, on hearing the guard say that the second was "forward."

A FACT THAT OUGHTN'T TO BE, BUT IS. Navvy. "As there's no room third class, mate, I suppose we shall have to put up with the fust."

MOST HORRIBLE. EDITOR OF "FISHBURY FULMINATOR" (in carriage). How's your circulation? EDITOR OF "BERMONDSEY BANNER OF FREEDOM." Oh! capital. How's yours? FIRST EDITOR. Well, not so good as it might be. The fact is, I want some good fresh blood; and I mean to have it, too. There's plenty to be got. Good bye!
[*Lady of full habit changes her carriage.*

LEX TALIONIS. Scene—*A Railway Station and 1,000 miles from Liverpool.*

PASSENGER (*to Guard*). I say, look here, you know, here's somebody here not smoking! [*Guard does not see how he can COPE with it.*]

SEEING OFF UNCLE HIGGINS.

I DON'T suffer so much from Uncle Higgins as some of the others do, so I've not the same reason for being so jolly glad to see him off. Yet I *am* rather jolly glad.

You see, Uncle Higgins is rather a dose. He's a bachelor, and his married sister and her two grown-up daughters keep house for him. He is very rich, and there is not the least necessity for him to go up to town every day to his office, unless it is just to worry the poor clerks. I have, however, no reason to think that this is not his motive for so doing, and he certainly does worry them. I am given to understand those clerks' lives are occasionally a burden to them.

I don't think the ladies at home are very happy. When Uncle H. comes home, he feeds plentifully, and has his glass or two of wine. He doesn't believe in that exploded old fashion, as he calls it, of the ladies leaving the room, and the gentlemen finishing another bottle. He finishes his other bottle when he feels inclined; but he doesn't like the ladies to go away.

He prefers cheerful converse. He drops off to sleep, and wakes up suddenly with a snort, and pretends he has not dropped off, but that he has been carrying on an animated conversation all the time. Woe betide that poor unhappy lady who falls asleep too, and is caught at it, or is even caught surreptitiously reading half a page of some book to while away the unutterable weariness.

Heavens! how much unutterable weariness goes to make up some women's lives! * * * * *

But there is just now joy in the house of Higgins! Uncle H. is going to the country to stop with an old friend for a month, and the poor suffering womenkind are to see him off, and I am of the party.

The servant is so long fetching the cab, there is a chance of uncle's not being in time for the train; so I volunteer to go in search of a four-wheeler with a fast horse. "How good you are, Mr. R—!" one of the poor women murmurs in the passage. "I am—I am," I respond with emotion. Goodness gracious! fancy his losing the train! He does not lose it, but on the way expresses an opinion that, after all, perhaps, it would be better not to go.

I shiver (for the poor things' sakes), and yet am fearful of advising either one way or the other. He's as obstinate as a pig! Presently, though, after painful suspense, he makes up his mind he will go, and we heave sighs of relief—covertly.

When we reach the station there is scarcely time to catch the train, but Uncle H. is in no hurry. Everything has to be done by rule, and as he pertinaciously sticks to his purse, we can do nothing until he passes the word—and the needful.

He has six packages, he says at the last moment; when on leaving the house, we counted them over twice, making five. Only when the bell is ringing he allows that he is wrong, and we rush him up the platform, and tumble him into the carriage. I own giving him a spiteful kind of nudge *en passant*.

When, at last, he has taken his seat in the carriage, we go through the counting again, and this time one of the five confounded parcels certainly is missing: it's his sandwich-box, on which, when I have run twice the length of the platform, and used grossly libellous language to all the officials, he is found to be sitting!

Of course, the train does not start as advertised, and we stand in a row outside the carriage door like a class at school. Uncle H.'s married sister says feebly,

"I hope you'll have a pleasant journey."

SEEING OFF UNCLE HIGGINS.

"Hate journeys!" he says; "I wish I'd never agreed to the thing."

"You'll write as soon as you arrive?" says niece number one, in a small voice.

"How am I to know when the post goes out at the confounded place?" retorts Uncle H., ferociously.

"You've got everything all right now," niece number two puts in, in a smaller voice still, but with a spasmodic attempt at cheerfulness.

"I suppose I have," he grunts: "you did the packing among you."

After this there comes a goodish-sized pause, and the three sufferers and I, afraid to be caught exchanging glances, keep our eyes resolutely fixed on vacancy. At length Uncle H.'s married sister—who, as a rule, is singularly unfortunate in her remarks—ventures to say, "The train's a long while behind, isn't it?" On which Uncle H. says, savagely, he is sorry to trouble us so, and adds, with a murderous glance at me, that perhaps Mr. R.'s time is valuable. On which I look at my watch, and say I've half an hour to the good before I need keep my appointment. (N.B.—I haven't got an appointment at all, and I know he knows I haven't.)

At last, as all torture must end, let you be ever so awfully martyred a martyr, the miscreant who has the doing of these things gives the signal we have been gasping for; and we all wave our hands to Uncle H., as the carriage containing him and his parcels glides swiftly along at the edge of the platform, and, taking a serpentine twist at the end, disappears from view.

Then, carried away by my feelings, I wave the forefinger of my right hand three times, and shout, "Hooray!" in a stage-whisper. At which facetiousness on my part Uncle H.'s married sister says, "How can you!" and the two other poor martyrs smile demurely with an appreciative expression, and all three consent, upon a little mild persuasion, to celebrate this festive occasion by partaking of a glass of sherry and a biscuit in the refreshment-room.

That evening there are jinks on a large scale at Uncle H.'s residence. Smith, an awfully funny fellow, who is in the Admiralty, and the two Miss Robinsons from the Crescent drop in, and I, too, am invited, and we have up some of Uncle H.'s most sacred port, and some champagne and other little things.

But in the middle of the dessert there comes a knock at the door, which most of us recognize with a kind of qualm, and one at least of the party (I refuse to name him) feels as though he would like to creep under the table and hide—if it were only a manly thing to do.

It is Uncle H. come back again! It would appear that after travelling all the way, he met his old schoolfellow on the platform, and then and there had a deadly quarrel with him—the cause of which is only vaguely described, but in which, however, it is quite evident Uncle Higgins was altogether in the wrong, and that he then and there took the next train back; and he says we shan't get him to go any more confounded journeys for some time to come!

* * * * * *

He has just asked me to pass him the port.

The married sister has an inspiration. She says, "Shall she fetch a bottle of the sacred?"—implying thereby that what we have got is the ordinary.

* * * * * *

It won't do. He says he will have what is on the table.

* * * * * *

IT IS AN ILL WIND, ETC. Well, then, if that nasty disagreeable old thing would persist in having the window down, was not Georgie compelled to put up her umbrella?

(But then about that fellow Jack? Ought he to have taken advantage of the circumstance? JUDY leaves the question to her lady readers to decide.

PENNY WISDOM. McCounter Jumper repents of an Easter trip in a third-class carriage.

NOT AT ALL UNREASONABLE. THOUGHTLESS YOUNG THING *with the skirt and bandbox (not used to travelling alone), who finds out her loss as the train is moving.* Oh! if you please, Porter, would you run and ask at the carriages whether I sat there, and if my ticket's under the seat? or perhaps the old gentleman who changed places with me is sitting on it.
[*Whistle—ticket lost for ever!*

UNKIND.

Boy. *Paper, sir?*   Swell. *No—can't read!*
Boy. *Get you a picture book, sir?*

THE DREAM AND THE AWAKENING.

Scene—*The Underground.*   Time—11.30 P.M.

She is young, she is fair, with an air
  That proves her well-bred and refined;
'T is late, and we two are alone,
  And—well, it is true—*I have dined.*

Long, long years ago, there was One;
  She brings back the thought of her face!
The same dreamy look in the eyes,
  The same indefinable grace.

Dead leaves lie thick o'er my youth,
  What odds now to curse or to weep?
I'm weary, and withered, and grey,
  And—surely I am not asleep!

"SORRY I SPOKE."

OLD LADY (sharply to stranger). *Well, Miss, what are you staring at? What do you see in my face?*

YOUNG LADY. *Nothing.* (End of conversation.)

This cannot be SHE! *She is dead!*
   Yet these are her lips and her breath—
As violets fresh from the earth,
   As in life—is it so then in death?

Her hand! How it stealthily creeps
   To nestle dovelike on my heart;
And there lies her portrait—she knows—
   I swore with it I would ne'er part.

My old love, oh! art thou then here?
   *   *   *   *
   I wake, and she's gone! So's my watch.
"Well known on the line," they tell me,
   "And one as we're anxious to cotch!"

THE VOW OF VENGEANCE.

A Story of St. James's Park Station.

It was a little podgy man,
    Uncommonly short in the leg—
"First-class, single, Westminster.
    And, oh, be quick, I beg!

"For I'm a Member of Parliament,
    And there's something on to-day,
And for a hundred thousand pounds
    I would not stay away."

They gave him a "first-class, Westminster,"
    And bade him turn to the right,
And told him they thought he'd better run,
    And run with all his might.

He ran with all his might, he did,
    And yet he was too late;
And in this M.P.'s face they banged
    Relentlessly the gate!

Then loud arose the M.P.'s voice
    O'er distant Big Ben's chimes—
"I'll knock you down! I'll lock you up!
    I'll—I'll—I'll write to the 'Times'!"

We who heard, we shivered and shook—
    Our faces blanched with fright!
We hied us home (at least, *I* did),
    And passed a sleepless night.

The red, red face of that little man
    Haunted me in my dreams;
I thought I heard his frantic cries
    Drowned in the engine's screams.

I waited a day—I waited two—
    Yet the world went on as before;
Then I went down to Printing House Square,
    And gave a rat-tat at the door.

The editor I could not see,
    The manager was out;
No one seemed to understand
    Quite, what I'd come about.

But I told a man I met outside,
    And he listened with a grin:
"He wrote that letter, I quite believe,
    But did they put it in?"

ROAD v. RAIL. GUARD. Going up by the express, sir? SWELL. Who? I? Not if I know it. I'm in a hurry; I shall drive.

IN TIME TO CATCH IT.

(SCENE—RAILWAY STATION, SOME DISTANCE FROM TOWN. TIME—11 P.M.)

JONES (who has promised the wife of his bosom that he will return home early that evening). *What time does the next train start for London?*

PORTER (playfully). *You're in capital time, sir—no occasion to hurry, sir—eight o'clock to-morrow morning!*

THEN AND NOW.

SCENE: *A Railway Station.*

THEN.

HE *to* HER (*with enthusiasm*):

    My pet, we're too soon or too late,
    And we have an hour to wait.
    I wish that that hour were two,
    To pass them, my darling, with you!   [*The hour passes.*
    Oh, bother it! here comes the train!
    I wish we could lose it again.
    [*Exeunt in opposite directions after elaborate leave-taking.*

NOW

SCENE: *The same Railway Station. Years are supposed to have elapsed.*

HE *to* HER (*with much less enthusiasm*):

    Confound it! as usual, too late!—
    As usual, too, we have to wait.
    What upon earth do you do?
    A person like you I ne'er knew!   [*The hour passes.*
    Thank God! here, at last, is the train.
    Well, you don't serve me this way again!
    [*They go away together: nobody helping any one into the carriage.*

AT THE SEASIDE.

RIFLE PRACTICE.

Shorncliffe is a very interesting locality, especially to mammas with marriageable daughters; in fact, for practice "from the knee," it may be said to be unequalled.

LITTLE PITCHERS. SHARP CHILD. I say, Mabel, what is that you are telling Captain Spoonie to "ask papa"? because he is just over there, and I will run and ask him for you if you like.

ENCORE UNE LUNE DE MIEL. Bride (to Happy Man, who can't breakfast). Dearest, we cannot quit this charming spot until we have hussed this volume, can we?
(There are two hundred more pages; but she had a couple of nice chops about an hour and a half ago, before coming out.)

A DEAD SET.

MAJOR GUMMY. *By Jove, what a bore! Here come those girls that are always making up to me, and I've got my confounded teeth in my pocket.*

SHINGLES AND SAND.

NEPTUNE is a greater autocrat than the Czar of all the Russias, but he has only got one surf.

YOU hear a good deal about the "Turn of the Tied." Some of them never turn: they haven't the pluck.

THERE is Smith, who, when in town, never seemed to know whether he was standing on his head or his heels, is down at Margate just now, and is talking of his 'and shoes.

ROBINSON, the eminent tallow-chandler (retired), is down at Scarborough. A friend asked him the other day whether he has always been in the habit of going so far for a dip? There's really no fun in this kind of thing! Dip-end on it, it's candlous!

THE ADVANTAGES OF TRAVEL. ANCIENT MARINER *(to Wander, a native of them parts)*. Ho, lad, an' I reckon they folks don't talk the same tongue up? Lissen to what they folks do hereabouts? HAWKER. Well, no. They don't say ho, lad: *they* say, Yes, sir. ANCIENT MARINER. And is Yes, sir, HAWKER. Ho, lad, it be. roight like?

DIVISION OF LABOUR. Time—Second Week of the Honeymoon. She. How provoking, dearest, that we did not bring out the next volume!
He. Isn't it, dearest? Suppose you just run back home for it. I'd better stop here, dearest, hadn't I? to take care no one gets our place!
She. And what will you do, dearest?
[*And the poor silly actually went.*

"UNREHEARSED EFFECT" in the life of a distinguished amateur actor, discovered in a secluded spot upon the South Coast by two ladies from the Theatres Royal, London, *without his "Air."*

NOT LIKELY. Tommy. I say, Auntie, the man says the salt water makes your legs strong. Is that true? Auntie. Good gracious me! how should I know? (Yet she hand been down to the sea every season for the last twenty years.)

Poor dear, much enduring Albert is at length allowed to take a kiss, but he can-

not manage it, after all, because of that confounded Dolly Varden hat.

"Oh dear me! there's that dreadful staring man again—and I have left my back hair in the machine!"

This is the dreadful staring man, with his spy-glass of fifty-horse power.

ROMANCE AND REALITY.—No. 1.
Here is the sentimental Alonzo gazing in rapture upon a footprint which he supposes to belong to the Imogen of his affections.

ROMANCE AND REALITY.—No. 2.
Alas! Imogen took a large-sized boot, and it was that podgy thing Aunt Betsy who wore such dainty *bottines*.

A "LOSER'S" NATURE. Scientific Party. How wonderful are the works of nature! This then is, no doubt, some curious specimen of the various littoral tribes which—— Young (?) Lady (*with acerbity*). I'll take my chignon, if you please, sir!

DESPERATE INCIDENT IN THE LIFE OF DEAR LITTLE MRS. WADDILOVE.

"No other way than that?—you low, common, vulgar boy, you! Ga' long!"

THE BROWNS ON THEIR TRAVELS.

At home in Brownstown the Browns are bad enough, but they're very awful indeed when you meet them out. You may meet them out every autumn.

There's Brown, senior: poor old man, at times you feel inclined to pity him. He would rather be at home quiet. Sometimes he employs artfulness, and sends Mrs. B. and the children down first. Then business keeps him a long while in town; but at last Mrs. Brown won't stand any more of Brown's nonsense, and she has him down. Serve him right.

There is young Brown, though, who married old Smith's daughter. They are both wonderfully well off, and young Brown has the biggest possible belief in himself, and young Mrs. Brown has the biggest possible belief in him also.

Young Brown is not tall, and young Mrs. Brown says she hates your great long lanky men. Young Brown is not personally beautiful, and young Mrs. Brown says she hates your pretty men. This, then, is all as it should be. I dare say even Brown himself would not alter if he could.

DREADFUL RESULTS OF SO MUCH FINE WEATHER.

The Honourable Johnny (cruelly afflicted). *Oh, Mith Mary, I'm tho glad I met you! Thith ith my little brother Billith, I thpoke about. We're having thuch a lark with our tubth and thpadeth, and we're going to take our thooths and thtockingths off directly. Will you come for a dabble?*

They come up to town from Brownstown on their way to the Continent, and put up at the Grosvenor, where they dine at a table set close to the window, and thoroughly in view of the common people in the street. They would not do such things for the world in Brownstown. To have their dining-room window-blinds pulled up ever so little would shock them excessively.

"But here, you know—passing through—where really no one knows one, it is quite different."

That's true enough of young Brown. We don't know him. He is a nobody here. I don't think, for that matter, he is much else anywhere. An obscure unit that is born, lives, eats, spends money, and dies, and there's the end of him.

Travelling on the Continent, he still keeps up his free and easy manners. He wears a billycock hat in the haunts of foreign fashion; but at Brownstown he would rather perish than appear in aught else but the highest and hardest chimneypot. He even goes without gloves occasionally.

TRUE LOVE AGAIN.
(AS USUAL, UNDER DIFFICULTIES.)

LATELY WED. *'Arry, dear, do take off your boots and carry me over, there's a duckey!*
BRUTE. *Likely! And I ain't a duckey, either! S'pose you take off yours, and swim over instead, to your own dear drakey-pakey.*
[*And this was their first outing only one year after.*

Pooh-poohing all he sees, mistrusting all he eats, he returns after a time quite eagerly to Brownstown, with the conviction stronger on him than ever, that he, Brown, is as near perfect as a male human creature can be, and little Mrs. Brown *knows* that he is right.

SHINGLES AND SAND.

FEW people think much about what the ocean takes away from us and what it returns. A respectable gentleman called Jones dropped his spectacles at Folkestone last year, and last week he was seen picking up the pebbles at Boulogne.

A GENTLEMAN took a machine the other day, and a header, and struck out. After a time, he did not return, and another gentleman struck out after him. No one now knows where the first gentleman went, but the second went to sea. Whether he saw or not, I cannot say.

A SUMMER STORY OF A SAIL AND A SELL. Inner Boatman (to Excursionist). Going out, sir? Columbined Excursionist. Have you got a match about you? Yes, I think so. (pretending he thought the poor man alluded to his pipe). (list the eager Boatman had not, and the Excursionist went upon his way with a chuckle.

"MEANING ME, SIR?"

SWELL (*pointing to the dog*). There's a little beauty, Frank! Miss Jerkinson (*mentally*). What a delightful fellow!
SWELL. And worth money, sir. Miss J. Oh, the horrid mercenary wretch!

PLEASANT FOR PENNYWISE. TOMMY AND FREDDY (*in a duet!*). Oh, ma', such fun! Old Pennywise won't pay—for—a—bathing—machine,—and he's—been—bathing—round—the—cliff,—and—we've—stolen—his—towels,—and—he's—trying—to—dry—himself—with—jellyfishes and seaweed! FREDDY (*solo*). Yes, and a star-fish!

RATHER HARD ON HIM, THOUGH. Poor old Puffles has married a dear scientific, strong-minded young thing, and they have been geologising in Cornwall, and she took him up awfully sharp just now, after splendid specimen, and he does not like to refuse just yet—during the honeymoon, you know.

CURIOSITY BEWARE! "*The cuttle fish is a curious animal, which even at pleasure project a dark brown liquid with great violence, against a wall —— imaginary foe.*" Young Adolphus Fitzdoodle is a curious animal who goes poking about other curious animals with his umbrella.

AND THIS IS THE GRATIFYING RESULT.

THE SHOP AT WINKLESEA.

Winklesea's rising. When first I knew Winklesea, there were only a coastguardsman and a pig in the place. The coastguardsman's there still, but they've found out the pig wasn't legal so near to human habitations, and the pig's great-grandson (the pig herself went baconwards) lives farther off down among the marshes.

I don't think he cares.

There is a terrace now at Winklesea, and the foundation for a square is being dug when the man and boy who have the job can find time; also an Assembly Room is talked of.

At present, however, the centre of attraction and principal seat of commerce in Winklesea is the shop. You can buy what you like at the shop if it's kept in stock. I won't say there's every novelty to be got there just as soon as you can get it in some of the shops in your Regent Street—but there's crinoline, anyhow. There are drapery goods and millinery for the fair sex, and there is cheese and bacon (one side of the pig's great-grandmother was sold here) for the consumption of both sexes. The fair sex down at Winklesea eat heartily, and even girls in love have "a twist on them," as the local saying is. This is supposed to be in consequence of the bracing sea-breezes.

THE SHOP AT WINKLESEA.

There are also toys sold at the shop, because babies are rather plentiful at Winklesea; and rattles, jumping jacks, and improved Mavors have been provided, to meet every emergency as time rolls on.

The proprietor of the shop also shaves. I won't say it's the very easiest shaving: I'd rather have the razors sharper if I had my choice, and you may over-do the angle in pushing back your customer's head, so as to get at him under the chin. You may get too near in, too, in search of the roots.

I've come away myself like the field of Waterloo just after the engagement; but I'm a peaceful kind of man, and bound up my wounds and held my peace.

I think it would have been as well if the Captain had done likewise. The Captain was a stranger at Winklesea, who came down and took No. 1 of the Terrace directly it was built, and long before the mortar was dry. (Mrs. Captain died of the damp mortar; but that has nothing to do with the case in hand.)

The Captain the first day came to the shop to be shaved. There were two of us waiting for our turns: one a native of Winklesea, and myself. The Captain came in blustering. He said, "How long will you be?" The proprietor of the shop is not a man who likes to be bullied, and he took his time answering; so the native of Winklesea hastened to observe that he was in no hurry to be shaved, and would give up his turn; and he felt sure I was in no hurry, and would give mine up too.

I don't quite like it to be thought that my time is of no value; but I am a quiet man, and I gave my turn up. The Captain, in spite of this, fumed and fretted, and I think this made the proprietor of the shop rather slower than usual. At last, however, the Captain got lathered—thoroughly well lathered—both ears full; and then there came a ring at the shop-bell. It was somebody wanting to buy a jumping jack.

The proprietor of the shop does not keep an assistant, so of course there was no one else to serve the jumping jack but himself, and nothing else to do but to leave the Captain with the lather drying on him, whilst he went to serve his other customer.

But the other customer was not going to be polished off directly with the first jumping jack that came to hand. He wanted to make a selection before parting with his penny, and the lather on the Captain dried into hard cakes and cracked.

Then the other customer said, after all, he didn't think he cared for a jumping jack that morning. He felt rather more like a tin whistle, and the stock of tin whistles were brought down; but then the Captain got regularly annoyed, and started up and stamped and swore, and called out to the proprietor of the shop,

"Look you here, Mister Shaver! Just you come back and finish shaving me, will you—confound you!"

The proprietor of the shop never uttered a word. He came back like a lamb, and finished shaving the Captain; and the Captain gave him sixpence, but he gave the Captain no change.

"How much do you charge?" asked the Captain.

"Sometimes," said the proprietor of the shop, "I charge a penny, and sometimes I charge twopence; but when there's language to put up with, it's sixpence."

The Captain brought an action about the change, but he lost it, and he has left Winklesea since. Whether he paid his rent or not, I can't say. I think not.

SOME UNCOMMON OBJECTS OF THE SEA-SHORE.

DOMINA INGENUA (the Honest Lodging-house Keeper). *Will you have the mutton cold, sir, or would you like it made into a nice 'ash?*

DOMINA CANDIDA (the Candid Landlady). *Which its billions there is on 'em all over the place, and a precious good job it is they've gave it you no worse.*

SOME UNCOMMON OBJECTS OF THE SEA-SHORE.

OBEDIENS MARITUS (the Dutiful Husband, who brings down the leg of lamb from town, and takes nothing whatever to drink on board the boat).

BONUS PUER (the Good Little Boy). *Oh, if you please, sir, there's a vulgar little gal, sir, a-havin' sich a lark with your hat!*

SOME UNCOMMON OBJECTS OF THE SEA-SHORE.

HOMO MODESTUS (the Good Young Man who looks another way when he accidentally comes upon a young lady bathing).

JUVENIS URBANUS (the Polite Young Man who steps aside to allow a lady to pass him on the pier). *She might as well have said "Thank you," though.*

Here they are more done up than ever, going home again.

Here they are spending the next evening.

"ON A MAY-DAY MORNING EARLY."

THERE is no mistake about its being May.

I have paid a good deal of attention to May, considered in the light of a month, and I ought to know. I have ere now been Maying with Phyllis and Flora (nothing at all wrong, dear madam, and with implicit confidence placed in me by the young ladies' mammas), and I have had rheumatism and neuralgia. I have culled the early primrose (we were trespassing at the time, if the strict truth must be told), and very nearly came to grief. I have gathered May from precious prickly hedges. Don't talk to me! I tell you I ought to know.

* * * * *

There's no mistake about it being early.

I have an alarum clock which belonged to an early riser who died young, and no wonder. I have also a trustworthy soul in my employ who, when you rashly name an hour overnight, keeps you properly up to it in the morning from conscientious motives, and there she is at the door.

I was a nice kind of noodle to make this brute of an appointment, I must say. What on earth did it signify to me whether or not my old French friend should go to his grave under the impression that there was always a fog all over England, and that we had no green trees? Still, I hate exaggeration.

I don't object to spending a day in the country with my old friend; but why should he want to begin his day at such an unreasonable hour in the morning? Don't you call nine o'clock an unreasonable hour? Well, I do. To get comfortably dressed and down to Waterloo Station by

RATHER ODD.

BOY. *Box o' lights, sir?*   PARTY (half asleep). *No, thanks, I'm a teetotaler.*

nine o'clock, I have to get up at seven. Seven! As though any man, unless he were going to be hanged, ever expected to be called upon to get up at seven!

There she is again!

"All right. ALL RIGHT, I say! Are you deaf?"

I suppose it would be an unmanly act on my part not to keep my appointment. He is just one of those punctilious kind of fellows who would take offence if I kept him waiting an hour or so.

What a fool I was, though, to agree to this journey! But it was late at night; it was after a good deal of dinner, and, as well as I can remember, a few toasts. My friend Chose had to go back to Paris all in a hurry about some business, and would return again in a week and go with me to Richmond.

"Is it an engagement?" he asked.

"Most decidedly," I said.

"Will you be there?" he asked. "Can I depend on you?"

"This is ungenerous of you, friend of my youth," I replied. "Did I ever pledge my word and break it?"

"Never, never," he murmured, and he then embraced me *à la Francaise* with effusion on both cheeks.

I think I may congratulate myself on having been rather a fool that night, and —There's half-past seven striking!

It is extraordinary how tired I feel. I seem as though I had not slept a wink all night. If it had been four o'clock in the morning, now, I had had to get up, I could have done it without regret. I was wide awake at four o'clock, and remained in that condition until five.

The quarter to. Now for it!

SUGAR-PLUMS

RATTLETRAP & TOOTLETUM

PHIZ

ALLY SLOPER

JUDY'S HIGH JINKS

A BOOK OF COMICALITIES

POOR CHILD! WELL HE MIGHT.

FOND DARLING (to his dear Mamma). *I know what it is, ma dear, that makes me so tiresome—it's because I want a squirt.*

Here's the confounded water in my bath stone-cold again, if it ever was warm, which I doubt. That old humbug is energetic enough in banging at my door, but boiling a kettle is quite another matter.

"Oh, yes; I hear you! I've been up ever so long!"

If the man wanted to see the beauties of the country, why couldn't he have come at a more reasonable time in the year? That's what I want to know. Or why couldn't he have taken my word for it, without dragging me out of bed in this way?

It was I who asked him, though, now I come to think of it; but I did not purpose starting at such an hour. These Frenchmen are so unreasonable. They rush headlong at a thing: they did so in the last war, and see what came of it.

Again, Frenchmen are so wretchedly prejudiced and narrow-minded as regards this country. There's this man Chose, for instance. He puts up, of course, at an hotel in a street off Leicester Square. He plays at dominoes and drinks absinthe, at the dingy little *cafés* round about, during the heat of the day, when he is not having his lunch or his dinner, and he strolls in Regent Street when the gas is lit, and thinks the other promenaders represent the English aristocracy.

On the whole, since the death of Lord Chief Baron Nicholson, since the Cyder Cellars have been closed, and Evans's has got to be dull and respectable, he finds London *triste;* and though no absolute fog chance to come within his personal experience, he is thoroughly impressed with the fact that a tremendous fog envelopes all the rest of the land which he does not happen to be in.

HOW IT HAPPENED.

YOUNG BRUTE (at back). *This is the Lover's Seat, Jack, and here are the lovers. Everything's provided, you see, all gratis and free of charge.*
[But that interrupted Jones, and her chance never came again.

Well, there's no fog to-day, anyhow, and though it's disgustingly cold, the sun shines brightly. I'll show him.
"No, thank you, nothing to eat. A cup of tea! That will do."
Here is an omnibus which will put me down close to the station door, so I need not take a cab. "Room inside?"
No; it's full. Inside and out it's packed like a fig-box, with clerks of all kinds going to their offices. Here are the results of getting up at this unnatural hour. I wonder how the clerks like getting up. They seem pretty cheerful, yet they do it every day. Really, though, joking apart, *they do.*
The station at last. I'm twenty minutes late, by all that's confounded. What a fool I was not to take a cab! Nice fuss he'll make about this, I know. Hang him and his appointments!

* * * * * * *

Well, this is rather funny, I *must* say. This is almost comic. Here have I been waiting a full hour, and he has not thought fit to turn up. I call this a positive insult!

SENTIMENT.

YOUNG LADY (to the Loving One who has timidly made a request). *Why, Gussy, you great big stupid, what on earth do you want with a lock of my hair? I've got a whole chignon at home you can take away and wear next to your heart if it pleases you.*

Where's the letter, by the way, the fellow wrote to remind me—*remind me*, if you please, observe that!—of our appointment? Ah! here it is.

Good gracious! This can't be yesterday's "Daily Telegraph!" They wouldn't sell me an old one, with a circulation like theirs. This is the right day of the week, I'm sure of that; but, then——By Jove! he says the tenth here, and this is the eleventh!

He was waiting for me at nine o'clock—yesterday!

* * * * * * *

Days have elapsed. We have met. We have been reconciled. For the world I would not offend my oldest and dearest friend upon earth. To-morrow is fixed for our long-talked-of excursion in search of green trees, sunshine, etc.

* * * * * * *

We have been on this brute of a journey. If ever there was a fog!—But, confound it! whenever is there a May-day in this idiotic climate of ours without a fog?

* * * * * * *

We've had a jolly row, and he has gone back to his native country with all his convictions unshaken.

WELL, SHE DID HER BEST, YOU KNOW. Wife of Valued Contributor. You know your Jupy expects your copy by to-night's post—do, for

MISS VIRGINIA SINGLETON AT THE SEASIDE.

Musician *(sings).* The maids of Merry England, how beautiful har they-ay! Miss Virginia Singleton. Really, Emma, that man sings with great taste for an individual of his description. I wonder if I have any halfpence in my bag to give the poor fellow.

A BAY THIN HORSE. BATHING MAN. "Yes, miss, he is surprisin' thin; and if you was to see the corn he 'as, it 'ud be more surprisin' still." [*No doubt.*

ONE OF THE GOOD OLD SORT. Seafaring Man, *who lets out boats (to persons pottering with nets).* Well, what I says to a party a-hirin' of my boat's this 'ere: You may be drownded, I says, but you ain't bound to be, I says; and you ain't bound not to be, neither, I says, and that's what I calls logic.

ANOTHER OF THE GOOD OLD SORT. OLD SALT (loq.) So, says I to the Admiral (just as I might say to you) you arn't got ne'era bit of 'baccy, your honour? [*Volunteers don't take the hint.*
OLD SALT (*continues*) No, Ben, I arn't, says the Admiral (just as you might say to me), but here's a shilling for you.

OVER PARTICULAR. Nice Old Gentleman (sol.) Shall I take a dip in the sea? I can't swim, and it's rather chilly. But then again, a hot bath is rather expensive, and decidedly not refreshing. And thus has it been for the last forty years, and I have never been able to make up my mind.
[*Dies before he does it.*

WEATHERWISE OR OTHERWISE. First Boatman. What d'ye think of the weather, Bill? Second Ditto. Why, I thinks as you thinks. Jack. First Ditto. Well, and I thinks the same.

NAUTICAL SIMPLICITY.

Gentleman (*to Boatman*). You must often, I should think, get wet, do you not? Artless Boatman. Yes, yer honour, we does, wery wet, wery wet indeed; but i'm wery dry just now, yer honour, and no mistake.

WHERE IGNORANCE IS BLISS, &c. PAT (*with coat over horse's eyes*). Plase your honour, make haste and jump up, for not a peg will he stir if he sees the rotundity of yer. The sly baste's an admirer of the feather-weights, bad luck to him!

NICE LADS. Old Poggles, a martyr to rheumatism, tells his grandson and companions to be good boys and not get into mischief while he takes a quiet nap.

There is nothing more pleasant than to see people enjoying themselves. Fido has his penny chair as well as his master and mistress. They are all very happy; but Fido's mistress would be even happier still if she hadn't eaten quite so much lobster salad for lunch.

When Clapham comes to the seaside it turns its back on the sea and reads good books. Well, quite right, too, if Clapham likes to do so.

There are some Plucky Little Things who paddle their own canoes. All canoes aren't big enough to hold some of the Plucky Little Things, though. This idea is patented.

SOME MORE SAYINGS FROM THE SAD SEA WAVES.

They say they don't object to allow this old lady the use of their sands; but she might as well put her pipe out.

They say that they are really growing tired of the seedy loafer, the obtrusive Jew gentleman, Mossoo, and the made-up old man, and wish they'd stop at home.

They say that they can always sympathize with beauty in distress; as, for instance, with Miss Smith here, who left off her coil for the first time yesterday, and, happening to put up her hand, forgot she had left it at home, and thought it had blown off.

HOLIDAY SKETCHES.

Always dread the summer months coming on.

"Would you like to hear a recitation from *Hamlet*? Jolly fun for old Jawkins, the dramatic critic!"

Always has a month at the seaside. Wonderful how he can afford it!

Down for the day. "Oh, lor'! oh, lor'!"

"Doctor says you're ill, and must go in the country? Nonsense!"

Don't care what it costs him when he goes away.

Not a profitable customer.

"Far, far away, in some quiet country spot!" Very much so!

J. T. on the sands.

HOW MRS. TODGERS TACKLED THE OCEAN.

It began this way: Said Miss Codgers to Mrs. Todgers, "You've no idea what it's like, my dear. For goodness' sake, don't miss it!"

And so Mrs. Todgers went down by excursion train. "No room, mum? There's plenty. You'll be all right when you've shook down a bit."

HOW MRS. TODGERS TACKLED THE OCEAN.

"The ocean, ma'am ? Well, if you mean the sea, it's abart a moile off from where we stands when t' toide is in, and when t' toide isn't in, it's abart two."

The tide was out, but Mrs. Todgers made up her mind to go and meet it — so she tripped lightly o'er the pebbly beach.

HOW MRS. TODGERS TACKLED THE OCEAN.

Unfortunately, when the tide did come in, it came with such a rush, Mrs. Todgers hadn't time to come back quite as trippingly as she went.

Going home, she paid for first-class to avoid the "squodging." "You may keep your oceans for me," said Mrs. Todgers.
[*This is the first-class where squodging was avoided.*]

LITTLE THINGS FROM FROU-FROUVILLE.

Hen bird and chicks. Chuck! chuck! A *petite* Marquise playing at mussel fishing. Who would not be a mussel (unboiled)? Two young French noblemen going for a dip.

SEASIDE HATS.

The latest style—very light, and airy, and convenient, and all that sort of thing. Wants a face to suit it, though. Remember this is only a fancy sketch.

Ought to be put down at once. How is her mamma, if she's on the off-side, to see whether the deceitful little thing is reading her book or fixing the Captain?

SEASIDE HATS.

A very gushing style this—"awfully fetching," on the pier, when a gentle breeze is on.

This isn't a bad style, though, for some people. Built somewhat on the extinguisher plan. Great facilities for keeping one's eye on anyone.

THE EARLIEST NEWS FROM THE SEASIDE.

Au revoir, chimneypots!

Brown is just going down for a day or two without any stupid fuss or ceremony, and has packed his box as full as ever he can get it, but yet has left nearly all the absolute necessaries outside.

Jones goes a walking tour; observe him putting on his walking-boots the morning he starts. The feet will work down into them a little better, perhaps, after a mile or two.

THE EARLIEST NEWS FROM THE SEASIDE.

Private view of a pensive maiden upon the sea-shore waiting for the visitors to come, and tracing strange devices on the sand.

The first visitor has come at last. A darling creature—all heart!

Robinson means to go a tour on horseback. As soon as he starts he is off—that's one comfort.

VIEWS AT SLOCUM PODGER.

(As seen from a lodging-house window.)

Morning.   Midday.

Evening.

"A BIT WORRIED."

I MET a man I know one day upon the pier at Ryde, and it struck me he was not looking very well; so I asked him what was the matter?

He said, "I don't know; I'm a bit worried. My wife died last night."

This simple statement struck me as being almost singularly free from exaggeration.

Perhaps, whilst that man's wife lived, he had been a good bit worried—hence, by comparison, he was only a bit worried now.

OUT FOR A HOLIDAY.

A sea-rious ceremony :—Miss Tootsicums is introduced to Miss Poppums; both little ladies of the greatest consequence, belonging to the best society.

"It's very jolly down here, isn't it?" "We're very fond of one another, aren't we?" "Don't you think it's very hot?" "Aren't you beginning to get thirsty?"

"It's very dull down here." "There's no one to talk to." "It's growing chilly." "A little bit of fire wouldn't be a bad thing when we get home."

She enjoyed herself very much. And he!???? What does that matter?

SOMETHING IN THAT.

Mawworm. "You had best er throw away that cigar, my boy; it will do you no good.
Wise Boy. "Yah! Go on wi' yer old 'umbug! If I chucked it away, you'd pick it up!"

PLEASANT FOR YOUNG TUFTHUNTER

(*Who has been doing all he can for the last month to get into a good set at Scarborough, and has only just succeeded.*)

Old Gent. "Well, you know, we happened to drop on a visitors' list, and sed you down in it, so I says to your Aunt Betsy, here, I says, let's go too. It's so dull at them seaside places, when you knows no one; and the old girl says, 'I've nothink to go in,' so I bought her out of——"

MORE HATS.

The "great-grandmamma." And don't the great-grandchildren look nice in it? Bless their pretty faces!

A playful thing in one of the new seaside hats.   A sentimental thing in one of the new seaside hats.

Ramsgate Swell *(buying sand-shoes)*. I'm really afraid that you haven't got anything to fit me.

Young Shoemakeress. Well, sir, you see, you're rather awkward. You're neither a man's size nor a boy's size. You're what we call boy's full size. [*Swell feels smaller than before.*

Extract from Letter. "It wasn't so much his sitting down that I cared about; only, when it's two shillin's an hour, you know——"

Mr. Smith cannot afford to send his children out of town this year, so they take headers in the back kitchen.

"In this old chair my father sat."— *The Book of DAYS*.

ABOUT WOODEN SPADES.

WE have often heard speculations with regard to the future of the pin tribe; but I want to know what becomes of the wooden spades? This is really a serious matter, and ought to be looked into. The trade in spades at the seaside is brisk. Spades are bought, and taken on to the sands, and disappear. Are they taken by mistake? I can't think that. Do they fall the prey of juvenile depredators? and does the man at the shop receive the stolen goods, and take the stains off by a chemical process? The matter ought to be properly seen into this season. There is really, nowadays, so much time wasted in inquiries into things not half as important. I speak feelingly, because I have been put to some expense in spades. You may call my spades what you like for what I care, as long as you keep your hands off them! The very cheapest one costs a penny.

THE SELFISH LOVER.

SHE saw me off, she said "good bye!"
   And as she did she kissed me;
I thought a tear stood in her eye—
   I wonder if she's missed me?

When I come down next Saturday,
   She'll come to the train to find me;
I would not grieve to go away,
   If I'd left no man behind me!

A BAD CASE.

HEARING I was engaged upon a seaside book, a young man called on me with what he entitled a joke. He said, "Have you room for this one?—What's the best place for *tea*-totallers to go to?—*Urn* Bay!"

I asked him whether it took him long to do this, and whether any one helped him? and, if so, whether they used instruments? He said he didn't know how it came about, but he had been very uneasy since. I felt for the young fellow, and asked whether his friends would not take care of him, and bring him up to something more respectable? He said they inclined towards cheesemongery, but he himself did not find it congenial. Seemingly, here is another good young cheese-monger gone wrong!

TRICKS UPON TRAVELLERS.

Young Misery to his Uncle (who's never seen the sea). You want to know why the sea goes back, eh? Well, you see, the waves are caused by the little fishes wagging their tails; then they swim away in order to get caught by the fishing-smacks; and then, as they can't live without water, the sea follows them; this causes high tide and low tide.

[Uncle marvels at his nephew's knowledge.

It may be remarked that, though riding-habits are generally rather expensive, they can be much longer than walking-dresses. Take the charming thing below as a case in point.

THE EARLY TRAIN.

(She sees him off.)

"OH, John, *my* John! 't is time
    for us to part.
  Would you could stay, but it
    must not be so;
Say, have you learnt the list you
    have by heart?
  Come early Saturday; and
    now, dear——go.

"The ear-rings that you pro-
    mised you 'll bring down?
  Can you afford them? Don't,
    dear, if you can't!
My boots, dear, too, they're
    cheaper far in town.
  What! see you robbed, my
    dear; I'm sure I shan't!

"One moment more—remember
    Baby's socks;
  And then the groceries you 'd.
    better get—
They are so dear down here.
    The children's frocks;
  The leg of mutton: mind you
    don't forget!"

GUARD.—"Now then, sir, if
  you're going on!"

THE HUSBAND'S BOAT

(She expects his return.)

SHE waits and watches there—
    with eager eyes
  She scans the surface of the
    deep green sea,
Until—oh, joy!—afar off she
    espies
  The longed-for boat approach
    —"Oh! where is he?"

"Aha! that form. It is!" She
    smiles, and then——
  O'er her fair brow there passes
    then a frown:
"He has forgotten, stupidest of
    men!
  The leg of mutton he was to
    bring down."

[*But he hadn't. He had it in
  his bag; and she was so
  glad to see them both!*

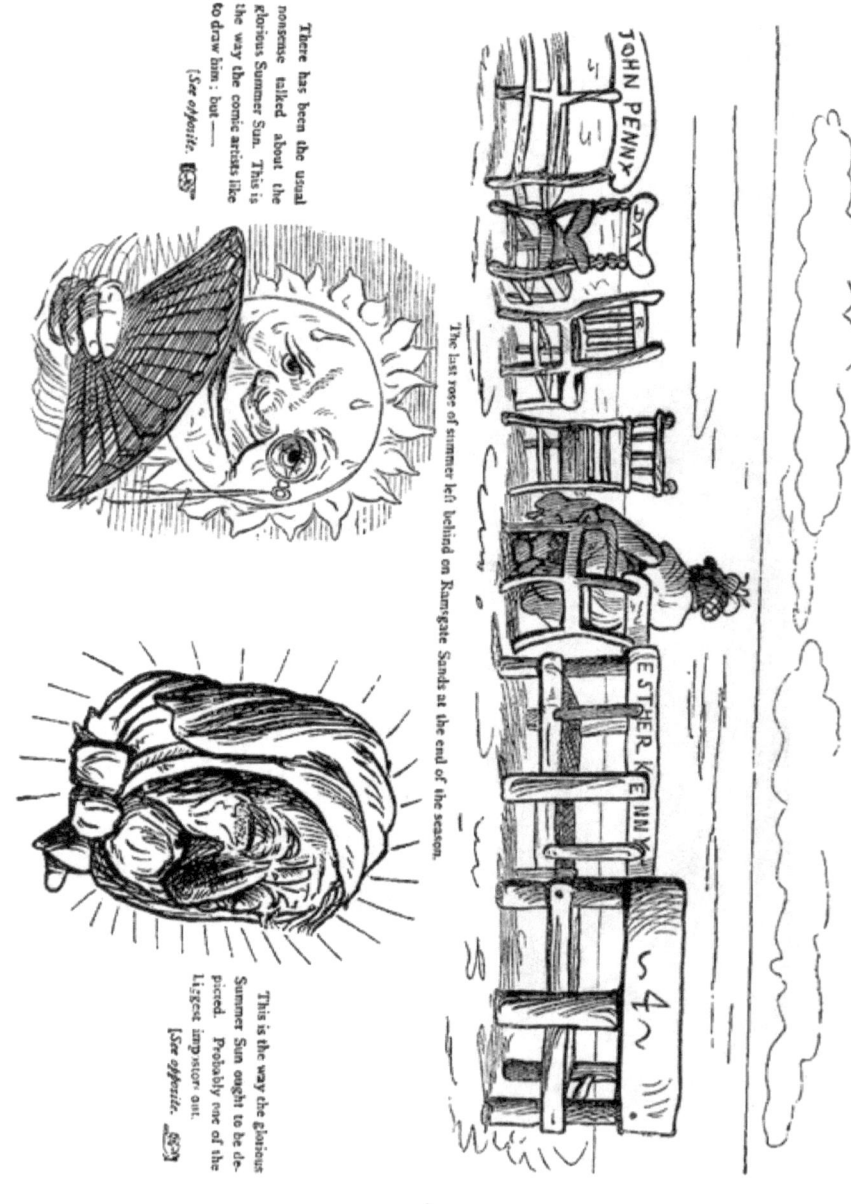

The last rose of summer left behind on Ramsgate Sands at the end of the season.

There has been the usual nonsense talked about the glorious Summer Sun. This is the way the comic artists like to draw him; but——
[See opposite.

This is the way the glorious Summer Sun ought to be depicted. Probably one of the biggest impostors out.
[See opposite.

THE FIRST LESSON.

LITTLE COQUETTE *(to common little boy on taking leave of the sands).* Yes, you *may* shake hands this once; but you're not to speak to me if you meet me in town, though; and, perhaps, if I come down next year, I may play at making sand-pies with you again.

The railway season has been extremely brisk and cheerful.

"Home, sweet home." So jolly to come back to it unexpectedly!

PROMENADES AND PIERS.

"COMING EVENTS CAST THEIR SHADOWS BEFORE THEM."

And it ought to have been a warning, only of course it wasn't.

A TRUE BILL. CLARA. What a hypocrite you are, Ellen, to pretend to be reading, when you know you're only looking out for young Spooninington. Well, then, why have you got your book upside-down? (*Ellen "gives it up."*)
ELLEN. What a story; I declare I am not!

AWKWARD! This is the Hon. Jack Bibber, one of the most gentlemanly creatures alive, even if he has been having a little extra (as is now the case), wondering which side of him the doosid dog's string is, and which leg he ought to lift up to step over it.

BOWLED OUT (and very properly too!) Arthur Whitedrake, Esquire, did not very particularly allude to the fact of his being a married man with a small family when he went en garçon out of town for a day or two. This autumn, by some dreadful blunder, he forgot that poor Mrs. W. had an invite from her maiden aunt for a couple of days, and happening to go down to the same place.—"By Jove, sir, I was regularly potted," said Mr. Whitedrake, describing the incident some time afterwards.

SHOCKING EVENTS. Elderly Lady *on seat (soliloquising).* Well! how those girls can be so disgusting as to make such an exhibition of their legs in broad daylight—etc., etc., etc. *[Goes home, and wonders how she could possibly have got another rheumatic attack in her lower limbs.*

"OH, WHAT A FALLING OFF WAS THERE!" Captain McDuffer (*of the Yeomanry*). Oh! yes, I was here on Easter Monday. I—I remember—of course—we saw you fall off!! Beauteous and Blown-away Being (*facetiously*). Ah! I remember—of course—we saw you fall off!! &c., &c., &c., *was mashed ashore*, &c., &c.—Next Morning's Paper. [*N.B.—The body of a gentleman*, &c., *was mashed ashore*, &c., &c.—Next Morning's Paper.

A SLIGHT MISS-APPREHENSION. ARABELLA. "What did uncle give you on your birthday, dear? he gave me 'Hard Cash.'" GEORGIE. "Half-a-Million of Money." INTELLIGENT FOREIGNER *(who has overheard the dialogue).* "Oh, mon dieu! but dese Anglaises are reecher as Crœsus!"

WAS IT LIKELY, NOW? IGNORANT FOREIGNER (*though perhaps, after all, he meant it otherwise*). Excuser, madame, but has it happen to ze back of your head to come itself off?

SEASIDE AMUSEMENTS.

WITHOUT FOUNDATION.

SEAFARING MAN (*telling romantic story*). *Yes, ma'am, and it was in that there wery boat as them two loving hearts escaped—him and her together.*
LADY VISITOR. *Bless me! Where did they both sit?*

A PLEASURE PARTY. This picture represents a boat-load, at a shilling a head, after the end of the first six-pennyworth. "Oh, Henry!" she said, "don't you wish they would turn back again?" But Henry spoke not.

How truly delightful to be accompanied down to Ramsgate by a man of gigantic intellect, who can point out every object of interest, and discourse thereon and enjoy his cigar——

Until after dinner and the North Foreland.

A WATER PARTY.
Now then, all together!!!

LITTLE JONES'S EXHIBITION.

ONE of the strangest hallucinations under which I have known the human male creature to labour, with the idea that he is amusing himself, is the hiring of a boat for a roaring day upon the water.

I don't allude to those persons who really know how to row, and, of course, those who not only know how to row themselves, but know how to swim when other people who do not know how to row upset the boat, are "out of it," as the saying is—figuratively and literally.

I have often wondered since the occurrence what in the name of goodness prompted little Jones to do what he did that awful day!

Jones (he is no more) was a pretty figure of a man—smallish, perhaps, as far as regards height, but broad in the chest, and with a voice on him which inspired awe.

It is good of Providence, it seems to me, to put big voices into little men, and let them thunder! Very often a loud voice goes further than a strong fist. You have read this, perhaps, in improving nursery works and elsewhere. You have seen how travellers' knees have knocked together at the sound of the giant's tremendous tones vibrating through the wood; and then how easily the giant was dispatched by the ingenious Jack when, presently, he made up his mind to do it.

However, I once knew a case which is not a case in point. There was a little man with a voice on him, who bullied a big man with no voice, awfully! He bullied him and badgered him for three hours right off, till the big man got very wild indeed; and then the big man doubled up his fist, and let the little man have it! He went in like an egg; and though the doctors took him in hand almost directly, and trepanned him here and there, and put him in a new back-bone (I won't

THE GOOD SAMARITAN.
(LATEST EDITION.)

KIND-HEARTED SAILOR MAN. *You take my advice, sir, brandy's the only thing to do you any good. You try and persuade my mate here to let yer have some—it's only a shilling a drop.*

---

swear to the exact operation, for I know little of surgery), he never was the same man again that he was before he got that one-er.

But, *in re* Jones, Heaven knows how he came to think he could row, and when labouring under that delusion, how he could have been so weak as to make an exhibition of himself, I cannot say. But he did.

"Look out for me," he said; "I shall row past your house."

The house in question overlooked the Thames, and behind the garden-wall we were all drawn up—that is to say, mamma and the young ladies and I; and one of the young ladies' heart was with little Jones, I may tell you, and her eyes were the first to perceive that manly form (he looked taller seated) as he appeared in the distance.

He gradually approached. I am no rower, but I thought he was a trifle splashy. He approached nearer. The row of us all beamed upon him brightly. He nodded and smiled, and passed on—a glow of triumph on his brow, and then—he caught a crab!—

The crabbedest crab you ever saw!—and his poor little legs flew about wildly like those of an impaled cockchafer. Even *she* could not forbear from a smile.

This would be a really funny story, I do believe, only just then a steamer came up and run down Jones's boat, and he was drowned!

VERY UNKIND OF HIM. It was all very well for that fellow Green Jones to pay for the dinner and stand a boat; but just how rude he happened to drop his twopenny-halfpenny new hat into the water, was that any reason why he should have upset us all? Some people are so selfish! Didn't the ladies speak their minds, though, when they got dry again!

OFF RAMSGATE, SEPT. 7. Tomkins thought he was fishing for cod, *secundum artem*. (*Vide iz'*) "*the tale*" *for the remainder of his visit.*

THEY MEANT NO HARM. The little boy said, "Here's the man that was fishing all day yesterday, and caught nothing." And she said, "I don't think he has caught anything again to-day." And the little boy said, "Poor man! do you think he has to catch fish to sell before he can get his dinner?" And the Lord Mahomey, who always will wear a shawl, said [...]

"THE PLEASURES OF HOPE."
Poor Gudgeons!

FISHFUL FANCIES.

How the deuce can you call fly-fishing the *gentle* craft?

THE roundest man I ever knew was an ang'lar.

WHEN a pair of soles are sent up for dinner, try and make one go all round—(never mind whether everybody has enough or not). You will then be able to refer to the one sent down again as the sole survivor.

IF you promise to treat a friend to a lobster salad, let it be a lobster salad. Don't crab it.

I AM not much of an angler myself; and when a facetious farmer whom I know told me there were a lot of perches in his paddock, I baited my hook and wired in at the pond in the centre. He meant the kind of perch that is sometimes called a pole! There's nothing like fun. This amused him and me for a good three hours, as well as some friends of his he brought there to have a look at me. I like fun!

BICYCLING EXTRAORDINARY.

WE were down at Johnson's place, and Johnson took Tallboys and me out on to the lawn and showed us two new bicycles he had bought, and asked whether we knew how to ride on them. The question rather tickled me, you know.

LEARNING HOW.

Tom. *Well, Charlie, how do you get on?*
Charlie. *Hanged if I know. I've only just learnt how to get off!*

I owned at once that I did not. There are some people who have time and inclination to learn everything; but it never entered into my wildest calculation to master the mystery of bicycling.

Tallboys knew, of course. He did not exactly say that he did. He made no remark; but when Johnson had vaulted into his seat on his bicycle, Tallboys went at his with every apparent confidence, and was down on his back on the other side before you could say "Jack Robinson." Johnson only said, "Hallo!" and Tallboys said nothing, but tackled the apparatus from the other side, and went down again with another crash! and Johnson said "Hallo!" again.

Then Johnson asked Tallboys to let him hold it for him while he got up; and Tallboys did; and they both went down this time. Then Johnson said, rubbing his head, "Look here, Tallboys! Have you ever been on one before?" and Tallboys owned he hadn't. "Look here, then, Tallboys," said Johnson, still rubbing his head, "let's drop it for to-day. You learn by yourself."

Tallboys has never, to my certain knowledge, had another try; but I heard him the other day telling another fellow any fool could master the difficulties of a bicycle in five minutes, and honestly he believes he could himself. There are some people like that.

NOT AT ALL EXACTING.

Fair Artist. Oh! Captain Spurs, you could so oblige me—— Captain Spurs. (enraptured.) D'lighted! Cha-w-med! How?
Fair Artist. Well, I want a fisherman in the foreground. *Will* you wade out to that boat?
[*And the Captain says* (aloud) Oh, certainly! *What he says to himself nobody knows.*

CIVIL ENGINEERING. The charge of the vectualling department at our picnic having fallen by lot to Flowers of the C.E., that is how we found him on our return from the castle ruins - his ready genius alleviating the ennui of waiting by securing himself a quiet nap.

A CASE OF MISTAKEN IDENTITY.

Short-sighted Maiden Lady (to rude buoy in the distance). *Ga-long with you, do! Ga-long, or I'll call the bathing woman, I will!*

"WHAT IS THIS ABOUT?" "Why, that poor dear Mr. Whuffles, innocent as an unborn babe of any guile, has taken it into his silly old head to read the newspaper on the steps of their bathing machine, and so the ladies——" "Good gracious, you don't say so!" "Yes, I do, and he kept them out there for full forty minutes."

A FLOPPER.

This is a young man who has just had his bath, and is waiting for the machine to be drawn in again.

This is the same young man, who did not hear the man call to him to hold fast. *Whew!*

THE BOYTON BUSINESS QUITE UNNECESSARY.

BATHING WOMAN. *Oh, no, ma'am, I think not, ma'am. I shouldn't be afeard, if I was you, ma'am—leastways, not of sinking!*

FROM BETWEEN THE BLANKETS.

I UNDERSTAND the sun is up,
    And that upon the sea
It's shining down refulgent—
    Refulgent as can be.

Strange that this does not move me!
    I don't doubt what is said;
But it strikes me I'm better
    Where I am now—in bed!

Some people wake too early,
    And some too early sleep;
Some would seem but made to work,
    And some but made to weep.

Bright sun! cease not thy shining,
    But keep a ray for me;—
Meanwhile I'll have my paper,
    And early cup of tea.

MORAL.—Always have your cup of tea brought to you the very first thing.

THE BATHING SEASON.
(JUDY SUBMITS TO HER LADY FRIENDS A FEW COSTUMES.)

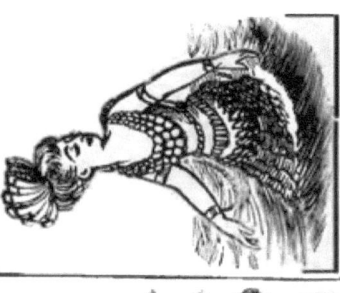

HISTORICAL.

This Picture of a gallant young English gentleman, who afterwards became a Lord High Admiral, is inserted for the special edification of other dirty little boys who don't like to be tubbed.

ON THE UNBECOMINGNESS OF MERMAIDS' ATTIRE.

I DO not mean what you mean.

I mean the modern mermaids of Splashton-super-Slop, young ladies of the very highest respectability, and wholly irreproachable, whose papas and mammas bring them down to Splashton for many reasons, one among the rest being that the sea bath may do them good.

I have nothing whatever to do with the class of mermaid persons Hans Breitmann describes as going about "mit nodings on." I allude rather to the Misses de Robinsons, four sweet girls, who, whilst I am speaking, have just gone out in one of Gore's machines, and presently will be flopping and floundering in the briny waves.

The proud purchaser of this enormous shillingsworth will doubtless be gratified by the contemplation of the pictorial embellishments, which as a rule are sufficiently truthful, and it even may strike the proud purchaser as being rather odd that I, who have been called upon to prose in the blank spaces where the pictures will not fit, should venture upon any adverse criticism upon JUDY's clever artists' spirited contributions — but I must; and I fearlessly assert that the mermaids' real attire is not half as becoming as it is here depicted.

A *sine quâ non* about a mermaid is to have flowing tresses; but the Misses de Robinsons' tresses have rather a rat-taily effect when they are wet, except, by the way, those of the eldest Miss de Robinson, who encases the back of her fair head in an oilskin arrangement, which keeps as much tresses as she has dry. Another *sine quâ non*, by the way, with the mermaid of fable, is a hand-glass, and I could forgive these dear girls if they took such a thing with them also, when they were getting unbecomingly tumbled, and absurdly red in the nose.

Have you ever noticed, dear Madam (I take it for granted you yourself are quite the reverse), how sure of itself, as a rule, is your adorable sex, and how little it notices?

The sweet de Robinson girls haven't a notion that their gambols with the waves (in truth, not a little calf-like and clumsy at times) excite anything but intense admiration in the distant beholders with field-glasses and telescopes. To float cloud-like and sweep majestically is the aim and end of much female ambition, and if the end be never reached in the generality of instances, the dear creatures, ten to one, never know it, and they never know, never, never ought to know, that the male observer knows they don't. The nonsensical pictures that French artists have, time out of mind, drawn of "*les baigneuses*" are absurdly, wilfully unlike the reality, and, oh! the rig-on-a-peg the loveliest loveliest often looks in the good old English style of bathing dress when wet, I tremble to think of.

My motive for making the foregoing observations is to persuade persons with forty horse-power glasses generally, to leave off. If I succeed I shall feel I have not laboured in vain — and shall then borrow their glasses.

Awful position of an ill-advised gentleman of retiring habits, who went out rowing all by himself and dropped an oar, and was driven by the tide among the lady bathers. "Go away, do!" — but he couldn't.

A SIGNAL OF DISTRESS. Terrible and appalling situation of Mr. Boffin on finding the driver of the machine overcome with the heat and fast asleep, the door bolted, and an evident uncertainness on the part of the horse to reach the Goodwins, or perish in the attempt.

A DREADFUL THING TO HAPPEN.

4. Awful event! He took a dive and came up right in front of her. That back hair, then, wasn't hers after all! and those curly black locks of his, too — the miserable old humbug!

5. Well might she fly. Well might he do ditto. Worse luck, though, they both flew in the wrong direction, and both got into the wrong bathing machines.

A DREADFUL THING TO HAPPEN.

6. What on earth are these? G-o-o-d G-r-a-c-i-o-u-s!!

7. And these, too. Very much more G-o-o-d G-r-a-c-i-o-u-s-e-r!!

8. They were obliged to dress in one another's clothes, poor things! But that wasn't all, either. The stupid, officious, dunderheaded local policeman took them into custody directly they landed.

SEASIDE ARITHMETIC. BATHING WOMAN. No, miss, fours into one won't go.

AWFUL INCIDENT ON THE SOUTH COAST. A short-sighted lady can't make out what on earth this board is about till she gets *quite close* to it.

HINTS TO LODGING HUNTERS.

Mr. Boffin is ordered by his medical man to seek repose at the seaside.
"They call 'em 'reposes,' do they? That's a new name!"

EVERYBODY thus employed must have experienced considerable difficulty in finding a good excuse for beating a retreat upon hearing that the rent of the lodgings they have been in to look at is too dear. One naturally likes to do anything else in the world rather than own up to one's poverty. Here, now, are two or three other excuses, which will be of very great service to you.

"HOW DOTH THE LITTLE BUSY B."

Well, it may "improve each *midnight hour*," but it certainly doesn't improve the morning countenance of our friend Bliffkins, who is on a visit to Margate.

1. Is there a church near?—No.—Oh, very well, then, you must live close to a church, so as to get there without inconvenience when it rains.
2. There is a church near.—That won't do, then.—You hate the sound of church bells.
3. Are there any other lodgers?—No.—You are very sorry, then; but, being of an extremely nervous temperament, you can't bear living in a house unless there are several men in it in case of accidents.
4. There *are* other lodgers.—Oh, very well; that won't do. You can't stand that.
5. Are there any children?—No.—Ah, then, you're very sorry indeed. The fact is, you dote on children, and having none of your own, your only object in taking lodgings is to obtain the occasional society of an engaging child.
6. There are children, are there? That's enough! Let's clear out of this!
7. With regard to dogs, the same arguments may be employed very effectively.

ABOUT DINNERS

FORTITER IN RE.

BRITISH GENTLEMAN. *Something for the Waiter? Why, I thought "waiting" was charged in the bill?*

WAITER (with presence of mind). *Yes, sir; but I think you'll find that's for your waitin' for the chop, sir! Yes, sir, thank you, sir.*

　　　　　　　　　　　　　[British Gentleman retires crestfallen.

SCRUPULOUS. PARTY (*who is particular about his wine*). Can you recommend your dry sherry? CONSCIENTIOUS WAITER. No, sir, I can't, sir—but the head waiter can, sir.

BEGINNING EARLY.
(A FACT.)

WAITER. *Can I get you anything, miss?*
MISS. *'Es, p'ease. A glass of bangy-an'-water.*
　　　　　　　　　[*Waiter is quite unequal to the situation.*

THERE are a great many more people nowadays than there used to be who look upon their dinner as a serious institution.

It costs money to dine.

There was a time—if one may take Dr. Smollett's word for it—when a needy gentleman, with a queue to his wig and a hanger by his side, could dine sumptuously for twopence-halfpenny, small beer included, if he chose to "dive" for it.

He had not got to dive into cold water bodily like a seal, and fish his dinner up from the bottom; nor had he to plunge a fork into a seething mess, and take his chance whether he got beef or boot-leather for his halfpenny. The dive he had to make was of another kind. Here and there in such neighbourhoods as Drury Lane, the doors of cellars stood open, and from the depths below savoury odours were wafted upwards to the street. The seedy buck watched his opportunity, and made a dash down the steps into one of these cellars, after the manner of people who would pledge their jewellery or personal attire entering one of Uncle Attenborough's establishments.

In the cellar below they found mixed company but excellent food—though I take it, the cleanliness of the cutlery and tablecloths was not made a great point of. I do not happen to know a place in London now where you can dine sumptuously for twopence-halfpenny, even exclusive of small beer.

I have a way of dining out and about three hundred and odd days in the year, and I know something of several kinds of public dining-places (restaurants they have of late years begun to call themselves), and at some of these I have suffered much, acquiring much wisdom also by the process, some of which I may perchance profitably impart for the benefit of other wandering gentiles in search of food.

I have no intention of saying anything at all calculated to do injury to the proprietors of the Sahara Hotel, but I should not care to dine again at their six o'clock *table d'hôte*. The Sahara is not affected by the highest quality, but is, nevertheless, vastly genteel. Our American cousins are thick as locusts in its coffee-room, and the luggage of county families goes in and out all day. It is a favourite hotel with most ladies, and the myriads of little cherubs in brightly bebuttoned liveries lend a peculiar charm to its domestic economy, and afford its fair visitors an opportunity of keeping much male servitude ever at its beck and call, running hither and thither to and fro incessantly.

I take it this is very delightful, and I think if I put up at the Sahara I should do likewise, or even more so, but I don't think I care about the *table d'hôte*. I won't say it is not served with every requisite formality, and that the waiters are not perfect in their way. I won't even say the *menu* French is very far out, but I don't care for *entrées*, the gravy of which is only just the soup warmed up again, and not well warmed either. Need I say more?

I have a dear old friend who comes to town annually at Cattle Show time, and puts up at Todd's in Sarcophagus Place, a stiflingly genteel hotel, very grand and dark, with patriarchal waiters, who fix you with a stony glare as you work your way through your three courses—and they are awfully particular as to the kind of fork you ought to use. I knew a man once (not intimately) who used a wrong fork for his fish. He died.

A fledgeling clerklet of my acquaintance tells me you can dine "rattling" at the famous establishment of Helterskelt's in Bucklersbury, and that he does so every day at one p.m. I don't understand how the adjective "rattling" can be satisfactorily applied to what ought to be a peaceful hour; but perhaps a person who dines daily at one, and survives it, may see no objection.

Really and truly, though, the wickedest and most heartless imposition is practised upon the poor Englishman with a taste for French cookery, who goes in search of it in London. Happily, my good friend Méchet, your little place is hidden away amidst impenetrable intricacies north-east of the square of Leicester, and no one is ever likely to find you out and come and bother me. I do not allude to your cookery, which happens to be good. But, oh! the frauds that have been perpetrated on me in my time by highly respectable impostors whom it would be

"WAIT FOR THE WAGGON."

TRAVELLER. *Well, what have you got to eat—where's the* carte?
WAITER. *Beg pardon, sir?*
TRAVELLER (impatiently). *The* carte! *the* carte!
WAITER. *Very sorry, sir, I am afraid we ain't got one. There's a dinner-waggin in No.* 4.

---

libellous to mention (shouldn't I like to!). The tinned peas of unkind flavour the stony-hearted *camembert;* the endless wickednesses; the messes à *la* kegmeg; the ice pudding, consisting of four pennyworth of Gatti and one pennyworth of preserved cherries! And, worse than all, the English-born-and-bred customers, who *will* ask for what they want in their French, of waiters who answer in their English on principle!—all which worries me somehow, though why, I cannot exactly say. Why is one more easily worried when "forty years over Michaelmas has passed," so much more easily, than one is twenty years younger?

Has it anything to do with one's digestion?

I believe it has.

In that case try——

On reflection, though—don't!

USE AND ABUSE. OLD GENT. You don't mean to tell me, Waiter, that you can't give me a toothpick? WAITER. Well, sir, we used to keep 'em, but the gents almost invariably took 'em away with 'em.

COOKSHOP ENGLISH. WAITER *(to Help).* Why, you've laid for two; there ain't nobody coming only him. HELP. What! has he only got hisself with him?

A DRY REJOINDER.

OLD SOAKER. *Ye know, I believe in the power of a fruity port.*
LIMB OF THE LAW. *Do ye now? Well, I believe in the power of a tawny.*
  [But whether he was really sunk so low as to mean "power of *attorney*," JUDY doesn't care to inquire.

A PARTING.

DON'T cry!
Don't cry!
Darling, we have to part!
Rest yet upon my heart.—
*   *   *   *
Now, good bye!
*   *   *   *
When next we meet, why, then—
Then! then——But when is *then?*
*   *   *   *
Never again!

FINIS.

Absolute Security against Burglary and Fire.

The "SICKER"
DOUBLE-GRIP BOLT SAFES, STRONG ROOMS, &c.,

INTERSECTED WITH
ADAMANTINE STEEL,
WHICH
NO DRILL OR POWER CAN PENETRATE,
And fitted with the Unpickable Duplex Locks.

The only Safes which cannot be opened without the Key.

Used in the International Exhibitions, and leading Banking, Bullion, Precious Stone, and Jewellery Establishments throughout the Kingdom.

PATENTEES AND SOLE MANUFACTURERS,
THE SICKER SAFE AND STRONG-ROOM CO., LIMITED.
WORKS—SOHO, BIRMINGHAM.
London—37 QUEEN STREET, CANNON STREET, E.C.

PAINLESS 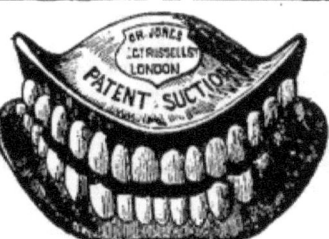 ARTIFICIAL

DENTISTRY. TEETH.

MR. G. H. JONES,
SURGEON DENTIST,
57 GREAT RUSSELL STREET, LONDON
(Immediately opposite the British Museum),
HAS OBTAINED
HER MAJESTY'S ROYAL LETTERS PATENT
For his perfectly painless system of adapting Prize Medal (London and Paris)
ARTIFICIAL TEETH BY ATMOSPHERIC PRESSURE.
Pamphlet Gratis and Post Free.

(TESTIMONIAL.) "October 18, 1873.
"MY DEAR DOCTOR,—I request you to accept my grateful thanks for your great professional assistance, which enables me to masticate my food, and wherever I go I shall show your professional skill, as I think the public ought to know where such great improvements in dentistry and mechanical skill can be obtained.
"I am, dear doctor, yours truly, S. G. HUTCHINS.
"G. H. JONES, Esq., D.D.S." "By appointment Surgeon-Dentist to the Queen.

RUPTURES.—BY ROYAL LETTERS PATENT.
WHITE'S MOC-MAIN LEVER TRUSS,

Perfected and Exhibited in the Great Exhibitions of 1851 and 1862,

Is allowed by upwards of 500 Medical Men to be the most effective invention in the Curative Treatment of HERNIA. The use of a steel spring, so often hurtful in its effects, is here avoided, a soft bandage being worn round the body, while the requisite resisting power is supplied by the MOC-MAIN PAD AND PATENT LEVER, fitting with so much ease and closeness that it cannot be detected, and may be worn during sleep. A descriptive Circular may be had, and the Truss (which cannot fail to fit) forwarded by post, on the circumference of the body (two inches below the hips) being sent to the Manufacturer,

JOHN WHITE, 228 PICCADILLY, LONDON.

Price of a Single Truss, 16s., 21s., 26s. 6d., and 31s. 6d. Postage free.
" Double Truss, 31s. 6d., 42s., and 52s. 6d. Postage free.
" Umbilical Truss, 42s. and 52s. 6d. Postage free.

Post Office Orders to be made payable to JOHN WHITE, Post Office, Piccadilly.

ELASTIC STOCKINGS, KNEE-CAPS, &c.
Prices: 4s. 6d., 7s. 6d., 10s., and 16s. each. Postage free.

CHEST EXPANDING BRACES
(FOR BOTH SEXES.)

For Gentlemen they act as a substitute for the ordinary braces. For Children they are invaluable, they prevent stooping and preserve the symmetry of the chest.
Prices for Children, 5s. 6d. and 7s. 6d.; Adults, 10s. 6d., 15s. 6d., and 21s. each. Postage free.

JOHN WHITE, MANUFACTURER, 228 PICCADILLY, LONDON, W.

"LEATHER-MAKE"
SCOURED CALICO
IS THE BEST.

Ladies should send penny stamp for patterns, which are neither charged nor requested back. Carriage paid to any part of the United Kingdom on £2 worth. Special terms for Charitable Institutions. Address,

C. WILLIAMSON, HIGH STREET, LEIGHTON BUZZARD, BEDS.

WHISKERS, MOUSTACHIOS,
BALDNESS.

Many Hundreds of Testimonials from private persons, and Opinions of the Press (London and Provincial), prove the fact that an unparalleled success has attended LATREILLE'S system of producing Whiskers and Moustachios, and curing Baldness. Full particulars sent free of charge to all applicants, town or country.

ADDRESS:
LATREILLE & Co., WALWORTH, LONDON.

FRAMPTON'S PILL OF HEALTH.

THIS excellent Family Medicine is the most effective remedy for Indigestion, Bilious and Liver Complaints, Sick-Headache, Loss of Appetite, Drowsiness, Giddiness, Spasms, and all Disorders of the Stomach and Bowels; and where an Aperient is required, nothing can be better adapted.

PERSONS OF A FULL HABIT, who are subject to Headache, Giddiness, Drowsiness, and Singing in the Ears, arising from too great a flow of blood to the head, should never be without them, as many dangerous symptoms will be entirely carried off by their use.

For FEMALES these Pills are truly excellent, removing all obstructions, the distressing Headache so very prevalent with the sex, Depression of Spirits, Dulness of Sight, Nervous Affections, Blotches, Pimples, and Sallowness of the Skin, and give a Healthy Bloom to the Complexion.

Sold by all Medicine Vendors at 1s. 1½d. and 2s. 9d. per box, or obtained through any Chemist.

GOUT AND RHEUMATISM.

THE excruciating pain of GOUT or RHEUMATISM is quickly relieved and cured in a few days by that celebrated Medicine,

BLAIR'S
GOUT & RHEUMATIC PILLS.

They require no restraint of diet or confinement during their use, and are certain to prevent the disease attacking any vital part.

Sold at 1s., 1s. 1½d., and 2s. 9d. per box by all Medicine Vendors.

GLENFIELD.

THE QUEEN'S LAUNDRESS SAYS THIS STARCH IS THE BEST SHE EVER USED.

GLENFIELD.

USE
STEINER'S VERMIN PASTE
For RATS, COCKROACHES, etc.

Sold by all Chemists, in 3d., 6d., and 1s. Glass Jars, with Directions for Use.

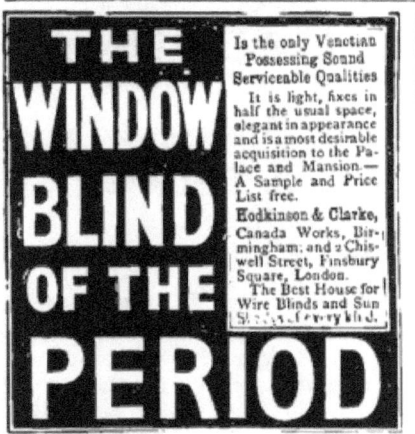

Is the only Venetian Possessing Sound Serviceable Qualities

It is light, fixes in half the usual space, elegant in appearance and is a most desirable acquisition to the Palace and Mansion.— A Sample and Price List free.

Hodkinson & Clarke, Canada Works, Birmingham: and 2 Chiswell Street, Finsbury Square, London.

The Best House for Wire Blinds and Sun Shades of every kind.

SEWING MACHINES ONLY 30/

Taylor's New Patent Twisted Loop Sewing Machine, a really useful machine for Thirty Shillings!! It makes the same stitch as the celebrated Willcox & Gibbs', is substantially constructed throughout, is mounted on handsome slab, so as not to require screwing to a table, and is fitted with all necessary apparatus, viz., Tucking Gauge, Self-Sewer, Hemmer, Braider, Oil Can, and Needles. It will Stitch, Hem, Fell, Braid, Bind, Quilt, Tuck and Gather, and do every kind of Domestic Work. The extraordinary cheapness of this machine brings it within the reach of persons of limited means, and also of those who, having a Foot Machine, desire a portable Hand one in addition. Wholesale and retail of the manufacturers, Taylor's Patent Sewing Machine Company, Limited, Driffield, Yorkshire, and 97 Cheapside, London, E.C.

"THE WONDER OF THE AGE." By Royal Letters Patent.

DR. J BALL & CO.'S
PATENT IVORY AND LIGNUM VITÆ EYE CUPS,

For the Restoration of Impaired Vision. All Diseases of the Eyes Cured under this safe and simple treatment.

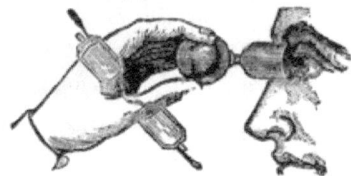

1. Impaired Vision. 2. Presbyopia, or Farsightedness, or Dimness of Vision, commonly called Blurring. 3. Asthenopia, or Weak Eyes. 4. Epiphora, Running or Watery Eyes. 5. Sore Eyes specially treated with the Eye Cups, certain cure. 6. Weakness of the Retina, or Optic Nerve. 7. Ophthalmia, or Inflammation of the Eye and its appendages, or Imperfect Vision from the effect of Inflammation. 8. Photophobia, or Intolerance of Light. 9. Overworked Eyes. 10. Mydeopsia, Moving Specks, or Floating Specks before the Eyes. 11. Amaurosis, or Obscurity of Vision. 12. Cataract. Partial Blindness, the Loss of Sight. Any one may use the Ivory Cups without the aid of doctors, and receive immediate beneficial results where our directions are carried out. Used only three minutes at night before going to bed. All instructions sent along with the Eye Cups. Enclose stamped envelope for particulars to

Mr. J. FLETCHER, Richmond Villa, Portfield, Chichester, Sussex,
Sole Patentee and Exclusive Agent for Great Britain for Dr. Ball's Eye Cups and Medicines.

A BEAUTIFUL SET OF TEETH.
JOHN GOSNELL AND CO.

Perfect Freedom from Premature Decay,

and Teeth of a Pearl-like Whiteness.

If you have never tried
JOHN GOSNELL & CO.'S
CHERRY TOOTH PASTE,
Do so at once, and you will never use any other
PREPARATION FOR THE TEETH.

If your Chemist or Perfumer does not keep it, you will greatly oblige by forwarding his name and address, with Eighteen Stamps, to

Messrs. JOHN GOSNELL AND CO., 93 Upper Thames Street, London,
And you will receive prepaid a pot by return of post.

Sold by all Drapers. "THE VERY BUTTON."—SHAKESPEARE.

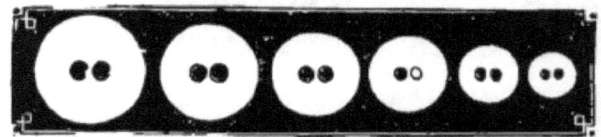

ASK FOR **GREEN & CADBURY'S**
PATENT LINEN BUTTONS.
BEWARE OF SPURIOUS IMITATIONS.

The name GREEN AND CADBURY is on every card.

SPRATT'S PATENT
MEAT FIBRINE
DOG CAKES.

Our success has caused a number of counterfeit imitations to be made, of highly dangerous and unnutritious ingredients. They are sold by unprincipled tradesmen as ours, for the sake of a small extra profit which the makers allow them.

Please observe that every Cake is stamped "SPRATT'S PATENT," without which none are genuine.

SPRATT'S PATENT
POULTRY & GAME MEAL.

The most successful Food for Rearing and Fattening Chickens, and causing Hens to lay.

Address—"SPRATT'S PATENT," Henry St., Bermondsey St., S.E.

DR. J. COLLIS BROWNE'S
CHLORODYNE
IS THE ORIGINAL AND ONLY GENUINE.

ADVICE TO INVALIDS.—If you wish to obtain quiet refreshing sleep, free from headache, relief from pain and anguish, to calm and assuage the weary achings of protracted disease, invigorate the nervous media, and regulate the circulating systems of the body, you will provide yourself with that marvellous remedy discovered by Dr. J. COLLIS BROWNE, Member of the College of Physicians, London, to which he gave the name of

CHLORODYNE,

And which is admitted by the Profession to be the most wonderful and valuable remedy ever discovered.

CHLORODYNE acts like a charm in DIARRHŒA, and is the only specific in CHOLERA and DYSENTERY.

CHLORODYNE is the best remedy known for COUGHS, CONSUMPTION, BRONCHITIS, ASTHMA, NEURALGIA.

CHLORODYNE effectually cuts short all attacks of EPILEPSY, HYSTERIA, PALPITATION, and SPASMS.

J. C. BAKER, Esq., M.D., Bideford.—"It is, without doubt, the most valuable and *certain* Anodyne we have."

Dr. M'MILLMAN, of New Galloway, Scotland.—"I consider it the most valuable medicine known."

CAUTION.—Vice-Chancellor Sir W. PAGE WOOD stated that Dr. J. COLLIS BROWNE was, undoubtedly, the inventor of CHLORODYNE; that the story of the defendant FREEMAN was deliberately untrue, which, he regretted to say, had been sworn to.—See *Times*, 13th July, 1864.

Sold in Bottles at 1s. 1½d., 2s. 9d., and 4s. 6d. each.
None is genuine without the Words "Dr. J. COLLIS BROWNE'S CHLORODYNE" on the Government Stamp.
Overwhelming Medical Testimony accompanies each bottle.

CAUTION.—Beware of Piracy and Imitations.

Sole Manufacturer—J. T. DAVENPORT, 33 Great Russell Street, Bloomsbury, London.

GREENSILL'S FAR-FAMED
MONA BOUQUET.
THE ORIGINAL AND ONLY GENUINE.
(Established 1852.)

The favourable reception and increasing popularity of this exquisite Perfume is a proof of its excellent quality.

T. S. GREENSILL, 78 Strand Street, Douglas, Isle of Man, bona fide Proprietor.

AGENTS.—LONDON: J. Sanger & Son; S. Maw, Son, & Thompson; Wm. Edwards; F. Newbery & Sons; Wm. Mather; Barclay & Sons; Whittaker & Grossmith. LIVERPOOL: Evans, Sons, & Co.; Clay, Dod, & Case; R. Sumner & Co.; Raimes & Co. MANCHESTER: J. Woolley; Lynch & Bateman; Jewsbury & Brown. EDINBURGH: Duncan & Flockhart. DUBLIN: M'Master, Hodgson, & Co. YORK: W. M. Thompson; Clark, Bleasdale, & Co. THIRSK: Wm. Foggitt. BRISTOL: Ferris & Co. LEEDS: Goodall, Backhouse, & Co. BIRMINGHAM: Mr. John Churchill; C. Britten.

Trade Mark—Tower of Refuge, Douglas Bay.

THE 'ALEXANDRA' CRESCENT FLOWER-HOLDER,

Made in the Finest Quality of Glass,

is THE Flower-stand of the season; it is novel and elegant in form, simple in construction, and is in the highest degree useful on the dinner and dessert tables. This charming novelty is made in several sizes, and can be purchased at most of the leading

CHINA AND GLASS WAREHOUSES

in the kingdom.

FIVE PRIZE MEDALS AWARDED.

GOODALL'S WORLD-RENOWNED HOUSEHOLD SPECIALITIES.

A single trial solicited from those who have not yet tried these splendid preparations.

GOODALL'S BAKING POWDER.

THE BEST IN THE WORLD.

The cheapest because the best, and indispensable to every household, and an inestimable boon to housewives. Makes delicious Puddings without eggs, Pastry without butter, and beautiful light Bread without yeast. Sold by Grocers, Oilmen, Chemists, &c., in 1d. Packets; 6d., 1s., and 2s. Tins.

Prepared by GOODALL, BACKHOUSE, & Co., LEEDS.

YORKSHIRE RELISH.

THE MOST DELICIOUS SAUCE IN THE WORLD.

This cheap and excellent Sauce makes the plainest viands palatable, and the daintiest dishes more delicious. To Chops, Steaks, Fish, &c., it is incomparable. Sold by Grocers, Oilmen, Chemists, &c., in Bottles, at 6d., 1s., and 2s. each.

Prepared by GOODALL, BACKHOUSE, & Co., LEEDS.

GOODALL'S QUININE WINE.

The best, cheapest, and most agreeable tonic yet introduced. The best remedy known for Indigestion, Loss of Appetite, General Debility, &c. Restores delicate invalids to health and vigour. Sold by Chemists, Grocers, &c., at 1s., 1s. 1½d., 2s., and 2s. 3d. each Bottle.

Prepared by GOODALL, BACKHOUSE, & Co., LEEDS.

DR. HASSALL'S FOOD FOR INFANTS, CHILDREN, & INVALIDS.

DR. ARTHUR HILL HASSALL, M.D., the inventor, recommends this as the best and most nourishing of all Infants' and Invalids' Foods which have hitherto been brought before the public. It contains every requisite for the full and healthy support and development of the body, and is, to a considerable extent, self-digestive. Recommended by the Medical Press and Faculty. Sold by Grocers, Druggists, Oilmen, &c., in Tins, at 6d., 1s., 2s., 3s. 6d., 6s., 15s., and 28s. each. A Treatise by Dr. Arthur Hill Hassall, M.D., on the "Alimentation of Infants, Children, and Invalids, with Hints on the General Management of Children," can be had post-free on application to the

Manufacturers, GOODALL, BACKHOUSE, & Co., LEEDS.

GRANT'S MORELLA CHERRY BRANDY

Supplied to Her Majesty at all the Royal Palaces.

GRANT'S MORELLA CHERRY BRANDY

Delicious—Wholesome—Sold everywhere. Refreshing with Aërated Waters.

GRANT'S MORELLA CHERRY BRANDY

MANUFACTURER:

T. GRANT,
DISTILLERY, MAIDSTONE.

☞ Powders and Pastes should be avoided, as they scratch the enamel and cause the teeth to decay. The

"PARAGON" FRAGRANT LIQUID DENTIFRICE

IS THE BEST IN THE WORLD.

IT MAKES THE TEETH BEAUTIFULLY WHITE, SWEETENS THE BREATH, REMOVES TARTAR, AND ARRESTS DECAY.

One trial of this delicious dentifrice will ensure permanent patronage.

OPINIONS OF THE PRESS ON THE "PARAGON."

The FIGARO says:—"Possesses many valuable qualities . . . and cleanses and whitens the teeth, while preventing discoloration and the accumulation of tartar."

The COURT JOURNAL says:—"Its excellent flavour cannot fail to please . . . and should meet with extensive patronage from the *elite*."

Sold in Bottles at 1s. and 2s. 6d., by Chemists and Perfumers throughout the World.

Sole Proprietor, **J. H. BOWEN,**
91 WIGMORE STREET, CAVENDISH SQUARE, LONDON, W.

FURNISH THROUGHOUT.

OETZMANN & CO.

DESCRIPTIVE
CATALOGUE
POST FREE.

67, 69, 71, 73, 77 & 79,
HAMPSTEAD ROAD,
NEAR TOTTENHAM COURT ROAD, LONDON.

HAIR DESTROYER.—248 HIGH HOLBORN, London.—ALEX. ROSS'S DEPILATORY removes superfluous hair from the face, neck, and arms without effect to the skin. Price 3s. 6d.; sent for 54 stamps. Had of all Chemists.

GREY HAIR.—248 HIGH HOLBORN, London.—ALEX. ROSS'S HAIR DYE produces a perfect light or dark colour immediately it is used. It is permanent, and perfectly natural in effect. Price 3s. 6d.; sent free for P.O. Order. Can be had in the Colonies by pattern post.

SPANISH FLY IS THE ACTING Ingredient in ALEX. ROSS'S CANTHARIDES OIL, which speedily produces whiskers and thickens hair, 3s. 6d.; sent by post for P.O. Order, 4s. Advice verbally or written, fee 5s. Letters by return.—A. ROSS, 248 High Holborn, London.

ALEX. ROSS'S GREAT HAIR RESTORER. Has no sediment. Restores grey hair in a few days. Produces a beautiful gloss. 3s. 6d.

A FACT.—ALEX. ROSS'S HAIR-COLOUR WASH will in 12 hours cause grey hair or whiskers to become their original colour. This is guaranteed by Alex. Ross. It is merely necessary to damp the hair with it. Price 10s. 6d.; sent for stamps.—248 High Holborn, London.

NOSE MACHINE.—THIS IS A Contrivance by which the soft cartilage of the nose is pressed into shape by wearing the instrument an hour daily for a short time. Price 10s. 6d.; sent free for stamps. A pamphlet, "Nose and its Remedy," two stamps.

ALEX. ROSS,
248 HIGH HOLBORN, LONDON.

OLEOGRAPHS & ENGRAVINGS

The largest selection in London,
at Reduced Prices; also,

FRAMES
of great variety.

GEO. REES.

**GEO. REES,
115 STRAND,**
AND
41, 42, and 43, Russell St.,
Covent Garden.

AQUABOSSOGRAPHS
ARE THE
BEST ENGRAVINGS COLOURED & EMBOSSED.
When Varnished, they will stand for 50 Years.

| GIVES RELIEF. FORMS A STOPPING. SAVES THE TOOTH. — Sold by all Chemists. 1s. 1½d. | **BUNTER'S NERVINE**
THE
INSTANT CURE
FOR
TOOTH-ACHE. | DESTROYS THE NERVE. PREVENTS DECAY. DOES NOT INJURE. — Sold by all Chemists. 1s. 1½d. |

ABYSSINIAN GOLD JEWELLERY

IS THE ONLY IMITATION which cannot be detected from "Real Gold Jewellery," possessing qualities so long needed and desired in Imitation Gold Jewellery, viz.:—Superiority of Finish, Elegance of Design, Solidity and Durability. It received a PRIZE MEDAL for its superiority over all other Imitation Jewellery. Catalogues, with Press Opinions, forwarded post-free on application.

SOLE MANUFACTURERS,

L. & A. PYKE, 32 ELY PLACE, HOLBORN.

City Depots:—153 Cheapside, 153a Cheapside, 68 Fleet Street.

WEST END Depot:—ROYAL POLYTECHNIC, Regent Street.

And at ALEXANDRA PALACE, MUSWELL HILL.

YOUNG'S
ARNICATED
CORN & BUNION PLAISTERS

Are the best ever invented for giving immediate ease and removing these painful excrescences.

Observe the Trade Mark, without which none are genuine.

Price 6d. and 1s. per Box. May be had of most Chemists.

BE SURE AND ASK FOR YOUNG'S.

HOLLOWAY'S PILLS & OINTMENT

THE **PILLS** purify the Blood, correct all disorders of the LIVER, STOMACH, KIDNEYS, and BOWELS, and are invaluable in all complaints incidental to Females.

The **OINTMENT** is unrivalled in the cure of BAD LEGS, OLD WOUNDS, SORES, and ULCERS.

For BRONCHITIS, DIPHTHERIA, GOUT, RHEUMATISM, and all Skin Diseases, its effect is miraculous.

STANLEY, GIBBONS & CO.'S PUBLICATIONS

THE IMPROVED POSTAGE STAMP ALBUMS. Price 1s. 8d., 2s. 10d., 3s. 9d., and 4s. 10d., post free.
THE IMPERIAL POSTAGE STAMP ALBUMS. Price 7s. 6d., 9s., 11s. 9d., 13s. 9d., 17s., and 26s. 6d., post free.
THE NATIONAL CREST ALBUMS. Price 1s. 8d., 2s. 11d., 3s. 11d., 5s. 6d., and 8s., post free.
THE STAMP COLLECTOR'S HANDBOOK. Full of valuable information. 700 Illustrations. Post free, 3s. 3d.
The Illustrated Price Catalogue, completely revised, post free, 2d.
PRICES OF PACKETS OF USED STAMPS.—No. 1 (100), 6d. No. 2 (50), 1s. No. 3 (12), 6d. No. 4 (50), 1s. No. 5 (25), 1s. No. 6 (100), 1s. 6d. No. 7 (100), 2s. No. 8 (100), 5s. No. 9 (200), 5s. No. 10 (100), 10s. No. 11 (700), 21s. No. 30 (20), 1s. No. 31 (20), 1s. No. 32 (20), 1s. No. 33 (20), 1s.
PRICES OF PACKETS OF POST-CARDS.—No. 24 (7), 6d. No. 25 (14), 1s. No. 26 (25), 2s. 6d. No. 27 (6), 6d. No. 28 (10), 1s. No. 29 (20), 1s. 6d. No. 29a (30), 3s.
SHEETS OF STAMPS SENT ON APPROVAL ON RECEIPT OF POSTAGE.
Full particulars of all the above are given in the "Illustrated Foreign Stamp and Crest Prospectus," crown 4to, 8 pp., containing a variety of information valuable to Collectors. Sent to any address, post free, on application to

STANLEY, GIBBONS & CO., 8 GOWER STREET, LONDON, W.C.

ONCE A USE AND EVER A CUSTOM.
Persons suffering from HEADACHE, INDIGESTION, PAINS IN THE SHOULDERS AND THE BACK, GOUT, RHEUMATISM, and GENERAL DEBILITY, are particularly recommended to try

PARR'S LIFE PILLS.

They have never been known to fail in affording immediate relief.

SOLD BY ALL CHEMISTS.

MAKE YOUR OWN CHARCOAL, THE NEW CURE

for INDIGESTION and its terrible train of Diseases, BILIOUS and LIVER COMPLAINTS, Habitual Constipation, Rheumatism, and all affections of the Chest and Kidneys. Recipe for its preparation and use, together with a trial Box of CONCENTRATED CHARCOAL DIGESTION PILLS, sent free on application. Enclose Stamped Addressed Envelope to 'Manager, Sanitary Carbon Company, Nottingham.' Dr. Hassall says: 'Your Charcoal is pure, well carbonised, and being prepared with great care, is well adapted for medicinal purposes.'

GIVES HEALTH! STRENGTH! COMFORT! AND QUIET NIGHTS!

Dr. Ridge's PATENT COOKED Food

FOR INFANTS, INVALIDS, &c

TESTIMONIAL.—DR. BARTLETT, the eminent analyst, who was examined before the Adulteration Committee of the House of Commons, writes: "Gentlemen,—I have completed a very elaborate analysis of your food. It proves perfectly genuine, and the preparation it has undergone during the lengthened process of gentle heating prevents any liability to the hatching of animal life, so common among raw farinaceous foods. As food for children during and after dentition, the constituents contain the elements of strong flesh-forming nutriment; while for invalids the lightness consequent upon the time occupied in cooking must be a most valuable quality."—DR. RIDGE'S FOOD makes delicious CUSTARDS, BAKED PUDDINGS, and BLANCMANGES; it is also largely used for thickening Soups, Gravies, &c.

Sold by Chemists and Grocers everywhere, 6d. to 10s. 6d.
Manufactory: Dr. RIDGE & CO., ROYAL FOOD MILLS, KINGSLAND, LONDON.

KEATING'S INSECT DESTROYING POWDER.

Kills BUGS.
,, FLEAS.
,, MOTHS.
,, BLACK BEETLES.

PRESERVES FURS AND WOOLLENS FROM MOTHS.

THIS Powder is unrivalled in destroying every species of offensive Insect, and is perfectly harmless to the smallest animal or bird.
May be obtained from all Chemists, in Tins, 1s. and 2s. 6d. each, or free by post, 14 and 33 Stamps, from

THOMAS KEATING, St. Paul's Churchyard, London.

MADAME TUSSAUD AND SONS'
EXHIBITION, BAKER STREET.

"Most evergreen of Institutions."—*Vide Graphic.*

SPECIAL ATTRACTIONS.

MAGNIFICENT COURT DRESSES,
Designed expressly and made by the first Houses in Paris.

ALSO

300 Portrait Models of Celebrities and Distinguished Personages of Present and Past times,

Including H.R.H. the Prince of Wales; the Princess of Wales; the Duke and Duchess of Edinburgh; Alfonso, King of Spain; King of Portugal; and the King of Greece.

THE COMPLETE LINE OF KINGS AND QUEENS OF ENGLAND,
From WILLIAM THE CONQUEROR to QUEEN VICTORIA, in Chronological Order.

NAPOLEONIC RELICS.

Admission 1s.; Children under Twelve, 6d.; Extra Rooms, 6d.
OPEN FROM TEN IN THE MORNING TILL TEN AT NIGHT.

Travellers by Metropolitan Railway stop at Baker Street Station.

DO NOT LET YOUR CHILD DIE!

Fennings' Children's Powders prevent Convulsions,
ARE COOLING AND SOOTHING.

Do not contain Calomel, Opium, Morphia, nor anything injurious to a tender babe.

FENNINGS' CHILDREN'S POWDERS

For Children Cutting their Teeth, to prevent Convulsions, and quickly to cure Fevers, Fits, Sicknesses, Windy Gripes, Thrush, and other Diseases of Childhood.

SAFE TEETHING. *EASY TEETHING.*

These pleasant-tasting Powders, if occasionally given to an Infant or Child, will prevent their having half the Feverish Ailments children usually have.

During the critical time of Teething, one of these Powders should be frequently given.

FENNINGS' COOLING POWDERS will produce easy Teething, and prevent Convulsions and Thrush.

FENNINGS' COOLING POWDERS are decidedly the safest and best Medicine that can be given to all Infants and Children, as they do not contain deadly Calomel, nor anything else that would injure the most tender babe.

Sold in Stamped Boxes, at 1s. 1½d. and 2s. 9d. (great saving), with full directions.

Read **FENNINGS' EVERY MOTHER'S BOOK**, which contains valuable hints on *Feeding, Teething, Weaning, Sleeping, &c.* Ask your Chemist for a *free* Copy.

FENNINGS' LUNG HEALERS,

A certain remedy to cure Colds, Coughs, Asthma, Bronchitis, Influenza, Incipient Consumption, and other Diseases of the Lungs.

FENNINGS' LUNG HEALERS will quickly cure the most obstinate Coughs, and if taken with a basin of gruel at bed-time, will frequently remove a slight cold in a single night. They cleanse away all impurities and inflammatory affections from the Lungs arising from Bronchitis, Influenza, the Cough of Measles, Incipient Consumption, or any other severe complaint irritating the pulmonary surface. (See Fennings' "Everybody's Doctor," page 15.)

Sold by all respectable Chemists in Stamped Boxes, at 1s. 1½d. and 2s. 9d., with full directions. The large-sized boxes, 2s. 9d., contains three times the quantity of the small boxes.

CHOLERA CURED.

SORE THROATS CURED WITH ONE DOSE. SCARLET and TYPHUS FEVER PREVENTED OR CURED.

FENNINGS' FEVER CURER,
OR,
FENNINGS' STOMACHIC MIXTURE.

BOWEL COMPLAINTS cured with One Dose.
TYPHUS or LOW FEVER cured with Two Doses.
DIPHTHERIA cured with Three Doses.
SCARLET FEVER cured with Four Doses.
CHOLERA cured with Five Doses.

A Dose taken twice a week will prevent a person catching Scarlet or Typhus Fever, or any infectious complaint, if in the neighbourhood or house.

Sold in bottles, 1s. 1½d. each, with full directions, by all Chemists.

Observe the Proprietor's name—ALFRED FENNINGS—printed on the Government Stamp round each Bottle, without which none are genuine.

Read FENNINGS' "EVERYBODY'S DOCTOR." Sent post-free for 13 stamps. Direct to ALFRED FENNINGS, West Cowes, Isle of Wight.

A box of Fennings' Lung Healers or Fennings' Children's Powders will be sent post-free upon receipt of 15 stamps, or 35 stamps, 2s. 9d. size, directed to

ALFRED FENNINGS, West Cowes, Isle of Wight.